The Movement of English Prose

IAN A. GORDON, head of the Department of English at the University of Wellington, is author of *Katherine Mansfield* and editor of *Shenstone's Miscellany, 1759-1763*.

The Movement of English Prose

IAN A. GORDON

Foreword by Randolph Quirk

INDIANA UNIVERSITY PRESS
Bloomington & London

Contents

Foreword

To the writing of *The Movement of English Prose*, Professor Gordon brings the rich experience of thirty years as Professor and Head of an important University English Department, and ten earlier years as a student and teacher in the University of Edinburgh. During this period he has been teaching the history of English language and literature, studying and writing upon the problems of doing so, and publishing the results of notable pieces of research into the work of writers as different as John Skelton and Katherine Mansfield. These brief notes on Professor Gordon's career constitute an explanation of his readiness to tackle so formidable and so rarely attempted a task as an analysis of modern prose from the standpoint of its long and complex history and in relation to the constant features in the fabric of our language from Anglo-Saxon times.

During this same period of forty years, there have been important developments in literary and linguistic scholarship which have deeply affected our assumptions and conditioned our thinking. They include on the one hand the thesis of the late Professor R. W. Chambers which insisted on the continuity of English prose, and on the other hand the emergence of modern linguistics with its special insistence on the analysis of spoken language and with the insights that have resulted from this. Such aspects of modern scholarship, shot through with a healthy controversy which is still with us, Professor Gordon has brought to bear on his accumulated reading and his intimate acquaintance with prose from the ninth to the twentieth centuries.

After stating in Part I the grounds as he sees them for continuity in our prose, the author proceeds with a chronological account of prose style from Anglo-Saxon times, singling out for enlightening comment and evaluation the chief exponents in each period, with carefully chosen examples which excellently illustrate the continuity theme while clearly drawing attention to the important variations introduced because of changing models, fashion, purpose, and language itself.

For the experienced reader, the book gathers a wealth of diverse information into a convenient survey presented with a unified viewpoint. For the less experienced reader, it would be difficult to imagine a more informative introduction – and for him the value of the book is enhanced by a concluding section containing exercises related especially to prose of the more familiar kinds written within the modern period.

University College London   RANDOLPH QUIRK
December 1965

Preface

This study, first planned as an opus, has by degrees dwindled into a book. English prose at the moment is so much in need of a fresh look that the original plan of writing up extensive field-notes, from explorations patiently done on the ground, has given way to what seems a more urgent requirement, a kind of aerial survey of the whole territory. The study of English prose as a medium of expression is beset with complexities, of which sometimes only the specialist is aware. The general reader, the critic, the philologist, and the structural linguist respond to the same page as if to different languages. Not the least of the difficulties is the time it takes even the professional to gain a working knowledge of a large enough range of texts to enable him to venture on an overall judgment. If anything useful is to emerge, one must resist certain short-cuts, notably the question-begging assumption that only important writers write important prose, and secondly the assumption that an area of English prose which for the modern reader is linguistically difficult or critically unfashionable can be safely ignored. Confronted with a library of texts and conflicting interpretations, the student needs a guide which will suggest the main lines of development without implying that all the answers are known.

The limits of this study, therefore, have been set not so much by scope as by scale. This little book is intended to be an introduction, written with coverage and compactness but (I hope) without superficiality, to a study where much remains to be done. My obligations to writers and scholars past and present are so considerable that only a general acknowledgment is appropriate in a work of this nature. I owe special debts to Professor A. McIntosh, Professor L. F. Brosnahan, and Professor Randolph Quirk for critical commentary, and to the Council of the Early English Text Society for permission to quote freely from the Society's publications.

University of Wellington   I A G
December 1965

Part one The Continuity of English Prose

Chapter 1

Preliminary Problems

The writer of a historical study of English prose is faced with problems unknown to the writer on English poetry. For the latter the territory has been charted by a series of explorers from Thomas Warton down to the last paperback or the last magistral volume from a university press. The brief history of poetry is confined to the major poets; the multi-volume history gives due space to the minors. Critical fashion, a lengthening historical perspective, or changes in sensibility may alter the status of this poet or that: the reputations of Pope, Donne, Tennyson, and Hopkins have shifted considerably in our own time. But though they may vary on the 'placing' of some poets, critics who adopt a historical approach present a united front, because they all proceed on certain tacit assumptions.

They have no difficulty in recognising what poetry *is*. It is what has been written by Chaucer or Milton or Herbert or Yeats. They do not differ among themselves as to who is or is not a poet. John Clare, Mark Akenside, Edward Benlowes may be of insufficient importance to find a place in a volume of two hundred pages, but the author is well aware that these men were poets. Equally, there is a notable measure of agreement on what a history of poetry should be. It has remained essentially a series of critical studies of English poets in chronological sequence. Critical fashion may differ on the amount of biographical detail that should be included, the amount of political or social history that should be given as background, the extent to which the temper of thought of a period, the intellectual and religious setting of the poet, are worthy of comment and illustration. Today, when even the value of literary history is denied by influential critics, literary histories, exclusively or predominantly a history of poetry, continue to flourish, all bearing a family resemblance to one another because they are based on the same set of tacit agreements.

The critic who attempts a historical study of English prose has no such comforts. Intensive work has been done in many areas – the mapping is almost topographical in its detail – but the whole terrain has never been charted on a uniform scale. The familiar sweep from *Beowulf* to T. S. Eliot finds no generally accepted parallel in works on the history of prose.

Do we follow the example of the historian of poetry and write a series of critical assessments of prose writers in chronological sequence? If so, who are the major authors? Malory, Milton, Swift, and Johnson? Obviously safe choices. There are others equally acceptable. Who – in a longer study – are the acceptable minors? Who, in prose, correspond to the Clares and the Benlowes and the Akensides? Who indeed?

Where does the history begin? 'The origins of English prose come relatively late in the development of English literary experience',[1] writes G. P. Krapp, who begins his *The Rise of Literary English Prose* in the latter half of the fourteenth century, a starting-point that found general acceptance until quite recently, when R. W. Chambers[2] argued persuasively for the 'continuity of English prose' from Alfred to the Renaissance. Chambers' views had, however, been anticipated in the nineties of last century by W. P. Ker – 'the pedigree of English prose goes back beyond Wycliffe and Chaucer ... it goes back to Alfred'. Ker's essay on earlier English prose,[3] buried in an outmoded anthology, has commanded little attention, and general critical opinion has acceded to Quiller-Couch's vigorous assertion in one of his first lectures at Cambridge[4] 'in words that admit of no misunderstanding' that from Anglo-Saxon prose our living prose has save linguistically no derivation. A recent popular and influential historical anthology, the five-volume *Pelican Book of English Prose*, in spite of Kenneth Muir's disclaimer in the introduction to volume one, 'English prose did not, of course, begin with the Tudors', nevertheless firmly begins at 1550, and so perpetuates a view of English prose that would have received the approval of Quiller-Couch.

By the mere choice of his starting-point, the critic who attempts a historical study of English prose involves himself in controversy at the outset. He has declared his belief (or his disbelief) that English prose before 1400 or even 1500 is part of the picture.

Many readers who accept a mediaeval or an Old English lyric as poetry – worthy of the same kind of consideration as a poem by Keats or Crashaw – almost unconsciously reject English prose written at the same time as the lyric as an affair for the linguistic specialist, a form not merely undeserving of but not even susceptible to the kind of critical attention merited by Swift or Henry James. The spelling, the vocabulary, the syntax, the uncomfortable unfamiliarity of the shapes of some of the letters appear to render it something entirely different from the medium used with such communicability by writers of the past few hundred years. For the great majority of readers, prose is only tolerable when its physical appearance on the printed page is up to date.

Herein lies a further and perhaps insuperable difficulty for the writer concerned with the movement, through time, of English prose, his only means of communication the printed page. Much English prose is, in essence, a transcription of the spoken word. It is possible to read aloud passages written ten centuries ago, and find that the spoken language of the earlier period still communicates to a present-day listener, who is puzzled if he merely attempts to look at the passage printed in its original spelling. Both reader and listener today can understand immediately the brief sentence in the story of the Prodigal Son in the 1611 Bible – 'And he arose, and came to his father.' The Old English version of the same sentence – 'Ond he aras þa ond com to his faeder' – looks in print like a foreign tongue. But the Anglo-Saxon sentence has the same words, the same syntax, the same word-order, the same sentence-stress. Read aloud immediately after the 1611 version, it is clearly recognisable. It is indeed the same language, though the values of all but one of the vowels and of at least one of the consonants have changed in the intervening centuries.

It is therefore necessary from time to time in this study to invoke the reader to try to get behind the unfamiliar look of the print and attempt to *hear* the words and sentences. They are usually more up to date than they look. The practice of ignoring the accidentals of older spelling and pronunciation has received universal sanction among editors of Shakespeare, who from Rowe's time to the present have consistently spelt his text as if Shakespeare were one of their contemporaries. Most present-day readers of Shakespeare are carefully protected against two shocks, Shakespeare's (and his compositors') spelling, and the pronunciation of English of the Chamberlain's Men. Neither would be acceptable today. The reader of older prose must be prepared to make mentally the kind of adjustments that editors of Shakespeare have incorporated into the accepted texts.

To be consistent with the above, it would be logical in this study to modernise spelling in all quotations. But this involves further difficulties. In almost every instance, the reader curious to go to the full text will find that the standard editions of prose authors (unlike the editions of Shakespeare) follow the spelling of the manuscript or the best early printing. Mediaeval authors are, of course, usually printed literatim from the manuscript, except for 'normalised' excerpts in students' handbooks. Were I to modernise spelling consistently, my illustrations might make the reader's transition to more extended reading in the end the more difficult.

There are also, as will appear, certain other advantages in retaining older spellings. The nettle must be grasped, and generally I have done so boldly, quoting from the 'original' spelling. But on occasion it has served my purpose better to modernise the spelling. Where this has been done, it is indicated clearly by adding the sign '(mod. sp.)'.

Any modernisation that occurs in succeeding pages will be confined to spelling. A text which attempts to go further and modernises words or forms by 'translation' into present-day 'equivalents' introduces inevitable falsification. It would imply that only words not readily recognisable have undergone semantic shifts. The contrary is more often the case. Many of the words not immediately recognisable in an older text are words for ideas or objects which have disappeared with the passage of time. Often the most difficult-looking words are the easiest to gloss. 'Haubergeon', 'Farthingale', 'stomacher', and 'points' have disappeared from the language of today because we no longer wear them as articles of clothing. The *NED* will soon set us right, and the obvious unfamiliarity of the words will drive us to the dictionary. But the case is different when (to remain in the area of clothing) the name of the article is still with us. What are we to make of the heroine of an eighteenth-century novel who appears for dinner in her 'night-gown'? Usually the context will reassure us and suggest – and the *NED* will confirm – that she is dressed for company and not for bed.[5] But with many words only alert reading will rouse suspicions that the meaning is not that of today. Words like 'sad', 'silly', 'shrewd', 'domination', 'gentle', 'smoke', 'wit', 'sentence', all in good present-day usage with precise and specific meanings, have carried very different meanings in past centuries and a careful assessment of date and context is called for, to yield the meaning proper for a particular text.

It is not the function of this book to discuss such semantic shifts, but a by-product of the historical study of English prose must be a continuous awareness of semantic history. The retention of the 'original' spelling is here of considerable assistance. When Sir Ector (in Malory's *Morte D'Arthur*) laments the death of Lancelot he says of him (mod. sp.), 'Thou were the kindest man that ever struck with sword.' Here the modernised spelling confirms that a fifteenth-century prose sentence is still good current English in rhythm and word-pattern. But the spelling also allays our semantic suspicions. 'The *kindest* man'? Kind men ('kind to animals' etc.) do not strike with sword. The spelling of the Winchester MS, 'Thou were the kyndest man that ever strake wyth swerde',[6] while it tends to make us forget that (vowel-changes apart) Sir Ector was using a modern English sentence, nevertheless does, or should, act as a warning signal. 'The kyndest man' was a man in the highest degree behaving according to his 'kynde' or nature, which by Camelot standards implied nobility of mind and bravery in battle. 'Kynde' in this context means predominantly 'noble/brave' and 'strake with swerde' is its proper correlative.

This clearing of the ground is but a preliminary to the major problem. A historical study of prose is a study of what? On the analogy of the standard histories of poetry (which are ultimately histories of poets and their work) it should be some kind of history of prose-writers and their work. By common agreement, one can identify the poets. Great or small, they all write something recognisable as 'poetry'. Can one similarly identify the prose writers, writing something recognisable as 'prose'? It is not impossible to make up a considerable list of such writers, on which there would be a fair measure of agreement. By ranging them in chronological sequence and writing a series of critical analyses of their work, one might produce a work of some interest. As a historical study of prose it would be inadequate.

'Prose' and 'poetry' are not simply different means of literary expression. The two terms are antithetical only within certain limits. Shakespeare and Donne write both poetry and prose. The choice depends on the circumstances, the audience, the genre – Anne More or the congregation of St. Paul's, the lyricism of Richard II or the middle-class mind of Mistress Page. Whichever medium is chosen, the writer is still the conscious artist. But there are great areas of prose which have no corresponding parallel in poetry, where the artistry is unconscious and incidental and usually is entirely absent. The domestic chit-chat of the *Paston Letters*, the bare narration of many entries in the *Anglo-Saxon Chronicle*, the cautiously observed experiments of Sir Robert Boyle – these are written in prose. If this kind of prose has no relevance, then the history of prose has already been written on many occasions as part of innumerable literary histories of England.

As critical terms, 'poetry' and 'prose' are not strictly parallel. 'Poetry' is simultaneously a description of a way of writing – covering a range of metrical forms – and a value-judgement. To say 'This is poetry' implies that for us what we read satisfies certain criteria – which may be aesthetic, moral, emotional, imaginative, and the rest. If the metrical work does not satisfy these criteria we have an alternative descriptive term at hand in the word 'verse'. 'Verse' has its own ambiguities as a critical term, but when used as the antithesis of 'poetry' it divides off a group of metrical writers, the versifiers who do not break through the sound-barrier that separates them from the poets. 'Prose', on the other hand merely describes a way of writing. As a critical term it makes no judgement. We have no separate critical term to describe prose which does not measure up to our criteria of excellence. We are reduced (as were Herbert Read and Bonamy Dobrée in their downright 'There is something immoral about bad prose') to the qualifying adjective.[7]

We make demands of poets which we do not make of users of prose. Poets, in T. S. Eliot's phrase, 'purify the dialect of the tribe', and we expect them to. All that the users of prose do is to speak or write the dialect. Some of them may purify it, elevate it into various literary shapes and attain an approved literary status; but while the poet is a member of a small minority writing for a somewhat larger minority, the user of prose is in the end everyone who knows the language. Prose (to cite Read and Dobrée again) is demotic.

A study of prose must be conscious of this enlarged range. Shelley and Tupper do not belong to the same species; *Areopagitica* and the cookery-book are sisters under the skin. Even if one attempts to limit one's consideration to the prose of 'literature', the prose of unadorned record and of natural conversation is often the ground-bass of the melody. From a context of almost cookery-book plainness and factual bluntness emerge some of the noblest passages of Anglo-Saxon; *Robinson Crusoe* on occasion reads like a ship-chandler's store list, and yet the same prose of virtually monosyllabic simplicity quickens to the magic of the discovery of the footprint; and where is one to draw the line between the court-records and depositions of quarrelsome Elizabethan gentlemen-scoundrels and the same scenes captured in the same idiom by Dekker and Deloney? The movement of conversation at various social levels, articulated into the narrative with varying degrees of literary sophistication, is the heart of the English novel, from Richardson and Fielding to Joyce and Virginia Woolf.

This, of course, is not the whole story. The casual speaking voice is not the only tone. The voice may be raised in anger or solemn exhortation or prayer; declamation, oratory, the sermon, the irony of the satirist demand a very different tone. A prose-writer like Jeremy Taylor or Milton may in addition call on the imagination and the imagery of the poet. The prose of Milton is often (though not always) a book prose, controlled by the structure of the written Latin of which he was also a master. But any consideration of English prose which is confined to the approved authors and the literary styles can tell only half the story, and even then leaves unexplained some of the excellence of the great writers.

The history of English prose must be regarded as a continuous development from its beginnings in Anglo-Saxon. R. W. Chambers' essay on continuity denied the idea of a 'break' in the Middle Ages. He argued that in spite of the official disuse of English from the eleventh to the mid-fourteenth century, prose on the Alfredian model continued in sermons and devotional treatises, and emerged triumphant in the English writings of Sir Thomas More and the successive translations of the Bible. The contention is valid and well documented, but it is not the whole explanation. The literary historian depends often too exclusively on documents. Documents do not in this instance constitute the whole or even the major part of the evidence. If it were so, we should have to accept R. M. Wilson's bleak verdict on the early Middle English period, 'English prose lingers on for some time but it eventually dies'.[8] What did die was the official use of English. English prose did not die but – in the language of the Resistance – went underground. The tremendous fact is that English survived, and re-emerged to become the language of literature and of power. It re-emerged because it had never disappeared. The continuity of English prose is a continuity of spoken English. The presence or absence of texts proves nothing against the weightier evidence, the actual survival of a rich and expressive language, with a sentence-structure that was modified and expanded but always without alteration of its essentials.

Speech is spoken before it is written. The student of English prose, though he is forced to base his study on manuscript and printed texts, must not allow himself to forget that up till the popularisation of printing, communication was almost exclusively oral. The older writer was conscious of the speaking voice and though he sets it down on paper or parchment he is writing for listeners rather than for readers. Anyone who has written a successful radio talk is well aware of the difference. Even when print became the normal means of dissemination, much prose remained oral in conception. The drama, the sermon, and the pamphlet (which can range from the Marprelate controversy to Newman's *Idea of a University*) perpetuate in print what was first conceived in terms of the spoken word. The essay and the novel seldom lose touch with the human voice.

But it would be a mistake to regard writing which is oral in conception as only a transcript of the spoken voice. Good prose of this type preserves the rhythm and shape of speech. It discards the garrulity, the loose ends, the amorphous form, the back-tracking and repetitions characteristic of most speakers. During an important period of our history many prose-writers went even further. They were not content merely to give shape to the prose of contemporary conversation. They studied and assimilated the more formal literary prose of Rome and to a lesser extent of Greece.

With Quintilian as textbook, and Cicero and Seneca as models, they elevated English prose to the grandeur of the late Renaissance. The baroque magnificence of the mid-seventeenth century was not to last. The prose of the past two and a half centuries has generally reverted to a basis of contemporary speech, though the lessons of the Renaissance were never to be forgotten.

This study, therefore, while it will draw most of its illustrations from the printed word, will on occasion remind the reader that behind the print is the voice. The evidence of the print is obvious and indeed tends to be overwhelming. There is more evidence for the 'voice' than the critic is often prepared to recognise. The English language and its history has been intensively studied in the past century and a half. Many of the results of this study have not yet found their place in the armoury of the literary critic. One of the unfortunate results of the common division between the 'language' and the 'literary' side of English studies is that practitioners of each discipline may forget that what they are studying is the same thing, the English language as a means of expression. Cultural history, aesthetic and emotional appreciation, close critical reading on the one hand, and the study of the word, the phrase, the sentence-pattern, semantic shift on the other, these are no more than different (but not alternative) ways of approaching English. Literary historian and critic ignore at their peril the findings of the older 'history of the language' and the newer structural linguistics.

The time has come to give an answer to the question posed earlier, and so to define the limits of this study. A historical study of English prose is a study of what? The remainder of this book is a consideration of the historical development of English prose as a means of expression. Though other aspects are given due weight, the emphasis throughout is on the structure of the English sentence. The title – the movement of English prose – contains a deliberate and, for my purposes, fortunate ambiguity. It is the movement of prose within the utterance, the sentence, the paragraph, the major prose unit. It is also the movement of English prose through time.

This is not a history of prose-writers, nor a history of what they wrote about. In particular, it is not a history of English literary prose, though the deeper understanding of all good prose is the ultimate objective. I hope to show that insight is sharpened and understanding of the qualities of good prose enriched by accepting a broader base and a longer history than is generally conceded. The remaining pages will attempt to justify and document this assertion.

Notes

1   G. P. KRAPP, *The Rise of English Literary Prose*, New York, 1915, v.

2   R. W. CHAMBERS, 'The Continuity of English Prose from Alfred to More and his School', in *Harpsfield's Life of More*, ed. E. V. HITCHCOCK, EETS, 1932.

3   H. CRAIK, ed., *English Prose*, London, 1893, i, 16.

4   A. QUILLER-COUCH, *On the Art of Writing*, Cambridge, 1916, 143.

5   *New English Dictionary*, 'night-gown', sense 2.

6   E. VINAVER, ed., *The Works of Sir Thomas Malory*, Oxford, 1954, 882.

7   B. DOBRÉE, & H. READ, *The London Book of English Prose*, London, 1931, xvi.

8   R. M. WILSON, *Early Middle English Literature*, London, 1939, 20.

Chapter 2

Continuity I:
Vocabulary, Stress, Segmentation

English began its life as a Germanic language. In its one and a half thousand years of recorded development it has shown, often at the same time, two apparently irreconcilable tendencies, a tenacious conservatism and a flair for innovation. Innovation, because it is the more obvious, has always had the fuller treatment. The history of the English language is almost invariably conceived as a history of continuous change. Such an approach is accurate – if one looks only at the changes. But there is a remarkable group of features in the language that have never changed. These permanent features of the language tend to be ignored and in many histories of the language are not even recorded. A field may be under crops one season and pasturing cattle the next. The change is considerable – to the casual onlooker. But it is the same field. Nothing has altered its contours or its subsoil or its basic geomorphic structure. The change is on the surface and many other similar changes will follow. Much of the conventional history of the English language records mere changes on the surface, and ignores the unchanging elements, the permanent contours of the language.

The changes have certainly been spectacular. The original inflected tongue lost most of its inflexions and its grammatical genders over a period of two hundred years. The vowels of Anglo-Saxon and many of its consonants changed and changed again. Diphthongs became simple vowels and simple vowels became diphthongs. A purely Germanic vocabulary was at first infiltrated and then apparently swamped by thousands of borrowings (odd term!) from Latin, from French, from Latin once more, and then from nearly every language with which Englishmen made contact. For some centuries now an English speaker or writer cannot express his thoughts with precision (let alone with any grace) without calling on the resources of non-Germanic Europe.

Had the history of English been merely a history of change the most intense scholarship would be required to read our earlier writers. In fact, the reverse is true. Apart from the ever-lurking snares of semantic shift, we can read texts written as far back as the sixteenth century without much difficulty. A little further effort will take us into the language of Chaucer. A modicum of the time necessary for French or Latin or Russian will give us an entry to the Anglo-Saxon of the tenth century – and what appears on first glance to be a 'foreign' language is seen on a closer examination to coincide in many essential features with the language of today. The most important of these essential features which have persisted with little or no change during the whole history of the English language are vocabulary, voice-stress with its associated phenomenon of segmentation, and a continuing array of phrase and sentence patterns.

Vocabulary

It was stated above that an Englishman cannot express his thoughts with precision without using words drawn from non-Germanic Europe. The wealth of our available vocabulary tends to obscure an even more important truism: without using our inherited Germanic vocabulary we cannot express ourselves at all. Many of the original Old English words disappeared. Many retreated from metropolitan and educated usage into class and regional dialects all over the English-speaking world. But a very considerable number remained; something like four-fifths of the original recorded prose vocabulary is still in active use. Most of our common words, the names of everyday objects and actions, the commoner adjectives and adverbs, the work-a-day verbs, the terms of family and social relationships, and all of the structural words in an English sentence (the pronouns, the prepositions, the articles, the deictics like 'this' and 'that', the auxiliary verb-forms that indicate tense, duration, possibility, capability and the like) belong to the original Germanic stock.

The importance of the Germanic elements in the vocabulary has been consistently obscured. The explicit Renaissance view[1] that English was an 'uneloquent' tongue that could achieve elegance only by borrowing heavily from Latin is still an implicit and unexamined premise in much educational and critical thinking. It is reinforced by a further Renaissance inheritance, the preference shown by the majority of critics for poetry rather than prose as the object of their attention. Nineteenth-century critics in particular were relatively uninterested in the structural excellence of a literary work and fastened rather on the inevitably right word or cadenced phrase as their Arnoldian touchstone. For them the 'inevitable' word was hardly ever a Germanic one. In Shakespeare's 'Absent thee from felicity awhile' or his 'multitudinous seas incarnadine' the classical words, cadenced and inevitable, shine like jewels. It is seldom the function of the native words to be so spectacular. Played by the pianist's left hand, they have a different job to do; but withdraw them, substance and counter-point are lost. When, as in recent years, criticism has expanded to consider a work as a whole, an interaction of words working together, each con-tributing to the full meaning, the native vocabulary, whether semantically significant or predominantly structural, assumes a greater importance. In good prose, where sentence-structure and not the use of the spectacular word is the supreme test of effectiveness and even of meaning, the im-portance of the Germanic elements is absolute.

This 'absolute' importance can be put to a simple test. Most English prose contains a certain percentage of non-Germanic words. If the per-centage rises beyond a certain critical point, even an educated reader reacts, and has always reacted, with distaste: in the Renaissance with the cry 'ink-horn terms' or 'Euphuism', in the nineteenth century with 'John-sonese', in Arnold with the damning though oddly inaccurate phrase 'Asiatic prose'.[2] The most classically conditioned reader feels there is a limit of tolerance. Beyond that limit lies pomposity, degenerating rapidly into mere burlesque. An English paragraph made up exclusively of non-Germanic vocabulary is structurally impossible.

The native words, on the other hand, can stand almost alone, on occasion entirely unsupported by non-Germanic elements. On such occasions they form a grainy textured prose that has over many centuries been a peculiarly effective way of speaking or writing:

> 'What!' quoth the Protector. 'thou servest me, I ween, with "ifs" and with "ands"? I tell thee they have so done, and that I will make good on thy body, traitor'. And therewith, as in great anger, he clapped his fist upon the board a great rap. At which token given, one cried 'Treason' without the chamber. Thereupon, a door clapped, and in came there rushing men in harness, as many as the chamber might hold. And anon the Protector said to the Lord Hastings: 'I arrest thee, traitor'. 'What, me, my lord?' quoth he. 'Yea, thee, traitor', quoth the Protector. And another let fly at the Lord Stanley, which shrank from the stroke and fell under the table, or else his head had been cleft to the teeth: for as shortly as he shrank, yet ran the blood about his ears.[3]

> It was from out the rinde of one apple tasted, that the knowledge of good and evill as two twins cleaving together leapt forth into the

World. And perhaps this is that doom which Adam fell into of knowing good and evill, that is to say of knowing good by evill.[4]

I would say to the House, as I said to those who have joined this
Government: 'I have nothing to offer but blood, toil, tears and
sweat.'[5]

The Germanic words in the above passages (from Sir Thomas More,
Milton, and Churchill) form respectively 91, 98, and 86 per cent of the
total words used.* These unusually high percentages are the result of the
writer's deliberate choice of native vocabulary, either regularly (with
More) or for specific purposes (with Milton and Churchill). But even a
longer, more 'typical', sample of the two latter writers shows a very high
percentage of native vocabulary. The Churchill passage from which the
above sentence is taken, although it is studded with phrases like 'lamen-
table catalogue of human crimes', 'former colleagues who are affected by
the political reconstruction', 'an Administration of this scale and complexity', still shows a 74 per cent occurrence of native vocabulary. The
page of *Areopagitica* which contains the Milton sentence, in spite of its
obvious foreign borrowings ('fugitive and cloistered virtue, unexercised
and unbreathed', 'voluntary imitation', 'immortal garland'), shows 83 per
cent of native occurrences. When a speaker of Churchill's terminological
exuberance needs three native words out of every four and a writer of
Milton's classical propensities needs four out of every five, one need hardly
document further the persistence and the continuing usefulness of the
original Germanic element in the vocabulary of English prose.

Stress

A second Germanic feature which has shown a remarkable persistence
throughout the whole history of English is voice stress. Germanic words
in isolation bore a strong stress on one syllable: longer duration, more
precise articulation and greater intensity of sound gave this syllable more
prominence. The remaining syllables were uttered less loudly and were
lightly stressed or unstressed. The stress system carried over from the word
in isolation to the word-group. Each word-group contained a point or
points where the voice achieved maximum emphasis, these major stresses
falling on the stressed syllable of words of semantic importance.

The use of stress in modern English speech is so automatic that it forms

---

* For the statistical basis of these percentages, see the discussion in Appendix A.

no part of the education of the native English speaker. In childhood, his pronunciation may need to be corrected, his use of forms and syntactical patterns almost certainly. But the rhythm of English speech, its moments of maximum emphasis, its secondary and tertiary stresses, its bundles of unstressed syllables, one must pick these up early or be unintelligible. It is perhaps strange that the feature of English to which least attention need be paid in the schoolroom is a major determinant of intelligibility. Those who have attempted to teach English to non-English speakers (particularly to those whose language is European but non-Germanic and most markedly to those whose language in non-Indo-European) are faced with this phenomenon at the first lesson. One can distort English grammar and still be intelligible. One can distort English vowels and consonants – murder the English language – and meaning still comes over. But distort the stress-system of individual words, ignore the stress-rhythm of the phrase and the sentence, and the result is absence of communication. An Italian or a French rhythm superimposed on an English sentence, combined though it may be with good grammar and approximately correct pronunciation, makes for difficult listening. The level stressing of some Indian or African languages superimposed on an English sentence produces a result which the native speaker finds hard to recognise as any variety of the English language.

It is significant that speakers whose native tongue is one of the Germanic languages find the least difficulty with the stress-system of English. The presence in all surviving Germanic languages of comparable stress patterns indicates an early common origin. The Germanic pattern of stressing, it can be inferred, was already in Anglo-Saxon when its various dialects were brought to England in the fifth century. It has remained virtually without alteration to the present day. More than any other feature of the language, it has led to a basic stability in English prose of every period. It is a real foundation of 'continuity'.

It is not always possible to produce convincing evidence for the sound of a language in earlier periods. It is unlikely, for example, we shall ever be able to say what English intonation sounded like in times past. But the stress-system of English prose can be documented very fully because it was carried over into the metrical practice of English poets and in some periods has been fully commented on by critical writers. It would be possible from the evidence of poetry to exhibit the stress-system of English prose of every period. Such elaboration is beyond the scope of this study. Two sample but important periods are adequate for illustration, the earliest (Old English) period and the Renaissance.

Old English versification has long since been analysed and though scholars like Sievers[6] and Pope[7] may differ in their technical descriptions there is no uncertainty about the rhythm of Old English verse. It was a rhythm that depended on stress. Regular emphasis or loudness gave it a recurring stress pattern, the pattern that was already present in the normal prose of the period. Stress in Old English verse (and hence in prose) was closely linked with meaning; the semantically important words were uttered with more emphasis. Nouns, adjectives, and the nominal parts of the verb (infinitives, participles) carried stress 'by right'; the finite verb was stressed when it was important for the sense; pronouns, prepositions, particles, conjunctions, and auxiliary verbs came low in the priority. Stress was carried on the root of the word, never on an inflexion. A prefix carried stress only when its meaning over-rode the meaning of the word to which it was attached (e.g. *ríht – únriht*, 'justice – injustice'). All that the Old English poet had to do to practise this metrical system was to formalise in half-line units and underline with alliteration the recurrent stress pattern of his ordinary language.

In Kemp Malone's words, 'verse rhythm was a heightened prose rhythm'.[8] With Old English versification as a guide we can turn confidently to Old English prose secure in the knowledge that our rendering of its stresses is based on something more certain than a subjective reading. The rhythm we discover is the prose rhythm of today:

þa   cóm he on mórgenne to þæm tún-geréfan
Then cáme he at mórning   to the tówn-reéve

þe   his eáldormon wæs; sǽgde him hwylce gífe
Who his álderman was; tóld him what   gíft

he   onféng; ond he hine sóna   to þære ábbudyssan
he (had) recéived; and he him spéedily to the ábbess

gelǽdde, and hire   þæt cýþde   and sǽgde
léd,   and to her it   disclósed and tóld.

The stresses in this Old English passage fall where we would expect them from our knowledge of the modern tongue, on the nouns and the verbs and the semantically significant adverb 'sona'. Instinct (which is here our imposition of modern reading habits on earlier texts) provides our guide. But the evidence from Old English verse furnishes an independent confirmation of the subjective and instinctive reading of the prose.

The stress rhythm of Old English prose is thus essentially the stress-rhythm of the prose of today. How was this preserved when English lost its dozens of unstressed inflexions in the eleventh and twelfth centuries? Had the inflexions sunk from light stress to zero stress without something taking their place, the characteristic wave-like pattern of English prose would have been replaced by a series of staccato heavy stresses, such as we find in contemporary newspaper headlines – 'Court Fines Girl Boy Friend Jailed'. The recurrent pattern of main stresses interspersed with secondary and lighter stresses was, however, preserved by the use of unstressed short words, mainly prepositions and auxiliary verbs, which took over from the discarded case-endings and verb-endings the semantic/grammatical function of indicating the inter-relationships between the more important words in the sentence. The basic rhythm of English prose was preserved. It had to be, because more than rhythm was involved. The rhythm of an English spoken sentence has always been part of the meaning.

One further example will demonstrate the stability of English speech stress. In the sixteenth century what can only now be described as a craze for classical scansion overtook certain English poets and critics: English verse was to be written in hexameters and other Latin metres; it was to be scanned not by 'accent' (i.e. stress) but by 'quantity' (i.e. duration of vowel-sound). *Forgiveness* was scanned by William Webbe (*A Discourse of English Poetrie*, 1586) as a 'Molossus, that is three long as – – –'. He cited with commendation and 'scanned' an English hexameter:

All trauellers doo gladlie report great praise to Vlisses.

Spenser flirted for a time with the fashionable innovation and Campion made it the subject of his engaging *Observations in the Art of English Poesie*, 1602.

The artillery of the opposition was soon brought to bear, the three most important texts being Puttenham's *The Arte of English Poesie*, 1589; Gabriel Harvey's *Letters on Reformed Versifying*, 1580 (in which he takes successful issue with Spenser), and Daniel's coda to the controversy, *A Defence of Ryme*, 1603. For the purposes of the present study the sixteenth-century controversy is complicated with side issues: the classicists, for example, wanted to discard rhyme as well as stress-scansion; the writers had no agreed common technical vocabulary and their use of terms like 'accent', 'long', 'short' varies from writer to writer and needs careful interpretation in the light of their examples.[9]

But one thing is clear. There was a critical outcry against anyone attempting to write poetry which ran against the natural stress-system of the language. Puttenham insists that what he calls the 'sharp accent' (i.e. the heavy stress) must come where it 'falls in our own ydiome most aptly and naturally'. Daniel calls for 'the true English reading and pronouncing thereof, without violating the accent' and condemns as 'unnatural' any forcing of the normal English stress into a classical quantitative pattern. Harvey, like the useful pedant he was, carefully marks the scansion of dozens of English words (e.g. bargáineth *not* bargāineth).

The controversy is now only part of literary history. But it provides us with unusually rich evidence for what was felt to be the 'natural' stress of the language of the time. From the evidence of these treatises (on both sides of the controversy) we can reconstruct the stress patterns of hundreds of English words used in the sixteenth century. In every instance, the stress corresponds exactly with that of today.

Segmentation

Stress, like the original Germanic vocabulary, is part of the permanent structure of the language. In addition, there is a third feature of spoken English for which one can find evidence from all periods. Not only is the modern spoken language stressed; it is segmented. The stream of sound is not continuous, but is produced and interpreted (though seldom consciously) as a series of separated word-groups. The boundary between each word-group and that following is marked by a transition phenomenon, the nature of which has been the subject of investigation and report in recent years.

This separation, by some kind of indicator between word-groups, is particularly noticeable in verse. Again, Old English verse is a useful pointer. Like all early Germanic verse, it was built from a series of units, two-stressed phrases or 'half-lines', which were linked in pairs by alliteration to make up a full line. In many early manuscripts (for example, the Junius MS of Caedmonian verse) the break between the units was marked by the scribe by means of a dot:

> Satan maþelode · sorgiende spræc ·
> se þe helle forþ · healdan sceolde ·
> gieman þæs grundes · wæs ær godes engel ·
> hwit on heofne · oþ hine his hyge forspeon · [10]
> (Satan spoke out sorrowing he spoke He who henceforth hell must hold Rule the area he who ere was the angel of God Bright in heaven till his mind seduced him)

This practice of marking 'breaks' persisted in Middle English manuscripts, and it survived into the early sixteenth-century printing of poetry, providing evidence stretching over several centuries that scribe and printer were attempting to indicate by a symbol something which they could actually hear. It is generally assumed that what they heard and marked was a pause, though it is conceivable (but not proveable) that the pause was associated with some change in intonation at the boundary of the word-group.

By the late sixteenth century, when treatises on poetry became common, the 'break' in a line of English poetry was identified without hesitation as a pause – in Sidney's words, 'That *Caesura*, or breathing place in the middest of the verse." [11] Puttenham, more technically sophisticated than Sidney, in his *Arte of English Poesie* was extremely knowledgeable about the nature of the break:

> The very nature of speach (because it goeth by clauses of severall construction and sence) requireth some space betwixt them with intermission of sound. [12]

He recognised that these 'intermissions of sound' could vary in duration according to their position in a sentence, and named three ascending values: the *comma*, the *colon*, and the *period*. For him the 'intermission' in poetry was only a special case of what was natural speech habit and prose practice – 'it appertaineth more to the orator or writer in prose than verse'. Puttenham was ahead of his time. What was implicit in the practice of Old and Middle English poets is explicit in his analysis: the movement of speech, with its stresses, its word-groups, its 'intermissions' between the word-groups, is the basis of both verse and prose.

The Old English half-line unit had a further characteristic, which has implications for any analysis of the structuring of Old English and later prose. The verse unit was a self-contained grammatical unit. It was either syntactically complete or, if not complete, was an understandable element the completion of which could be anticipated by the listener. When the ninth-century listener heard poetry, he heard what C. L. Wrenn has called 'merely a selection of ordinary prose patterns'. [13] He heard the series of stressed word-groups (each syntactically complete, each separated from the other by 'intermission') that he heard in ordinary prose; except that in verse the stresses were more emphatic, the 'intermissions' more marked. The stresses of Old English verse have already been used to suggest the stresses of Old English prose; the evidence of verse allows us further to postulate with some confidence the word-groupings and 'pauses' of an Old English prose sentence:

Dæghwamlice   man unriht rærde   ealles to wide
gynd ealle þas þeode   (Wulfstan)
(Every day   they have committed injustice   all too widely
in all this nation)

It does not seem accidental that the patterns both of stress and of segmentation correspond with those of today.

The development in recent years of strucutral linguistics has thrown light on the mechanics of modern English. The stream of sound can be recorded on tape and analysed at leisure; features such as variations in stress and pitch can be isolated by special instruments. Study of such recordings confirms what can be detected by careful listening. The stream of speech is not continuous. It is segmented into minor syntactical units, each of which has superimposed upon it a pattern of stress and intonation. Each tends to be separated from the succeeding unit by a transition phenomenon at the boundary.

In a sentence like, 'He went to the house', there is a slight prolongation of the final sounds of 'went', and this acts as a 'separation' between the first segment 'he went' and the second segment 'to the house'. This transition marker is commonly called a juncture. Junctures of this type represent the minimum degree of separation between word-groups. Three other separations, progressively more emphatic, are commonly recognised.

A conversational exchange like the following illustrates all four:

Do you like coffee? No – I prefer tea.

If one assumes that the first question is addressed to several people, then there is a stress on 'yóu' with prolongation, forming a juncture between 'you' and 'like':

Do yóu   like cóffee?

A more emphatic break (prolongation, possibly followed by a slight pause) appears after 'No'. Still more emphatic is the separation (upturn of the voice followed by a pause) after 'coffee?'. The terminal pattern (downturn followed by silence) after 'tea' is the most emphatic of all. Although there is an unfortunate diversity in nomenclature, most writers on linguistics recognise these four ascending degrees of separation at the boundaries between word-groups, and in one notation they are transcribed by the four symbols $+$ | ‖ $\#$. The segmentation can be transcribed thus:

Do you $+$ like coffee ‖ No | I prefer tea $\#$

In modern spoken English, segmentation, stress and intonation work together to signal meaning to the listener. The question 'Do you like coffee?' has three main stress-intonation-segmentation patterns, all with different meanings:

Do you like cóffee   ‖   (One person addressed. 'Yes' or 'No' are equally likely in response)

Do yóu + like cóffee ‖   (Several persons present; one is addressed)

Do you líke + cóffee ‖   (One person addressed; he is rather expected to say 'No')

The extensive exploration of English prose of earlier periods in the light of this kind of analysis has not yet been attempted. The correlations already noted between early and recent observations suggest that segmentation, like stress, is a stable feature of the language – Puttenham's three-point-scale for 'intermissions of sound' is a remarkable foreshadowing of what some recent linguists have named junctures, transcribed by |, ‖, and #, and others have described as the 'three clause terminals' or the 'three terminal contours'. The continuity (in the speech of successive generations) of the minor syntactical unit, separated from its neighbours by boundary-markers, goes a long way to explain what is discussed more fully in the following chapter, the preservation from the earliest to the most recent times of a whole series of phrase and complete sentence patterns.

Notes

1 R. F. JONES, *The Triumph of the English Language*, Stanford, 1953, Ch. I 'The Uneloquent Language', 3–31.

2 M. ARNOLD, *Essays in Criticism*, first series, 'The Literary Influence of Academies', London, 1865.

3 W. E. CAMPBELL, ed., *The English Works of Sir Thomas More*, London, 1931, i, 427.

4 *Areopagitica*, in *The Works of John Milton*, Columbia edition, New York, 1931, iv, 310.

5 *Parliamentary Debates*, 1939–40, vi, 1502.

6 E. SIEVERS, *Altgermanische Metrik*, Halle, 1893, is the source, but his system is common in all edd. of OE poetry.

7 J. C. POPE, *The Rhythm of Beowulf*, New Haven, 1942.

8 A. C. BAUGH, ed., *A Literary History of England*, New York, 1948, 10.

9 The texts cited are to be found in C. GREGORY SMITH, *Elizabethan Critical Essays*, Oxford, 1904.

10 G. P. KRAPP, ed., *The Junius Manuscript*, London, 1931, xxii–xxiii.

11 C. GREGORY SMITH, *op. cit.*, i, 205.

12 C. GREGORY SMITH, *op. cit.*, ii, 77.

13 C. L. WRENN, ed., *Beowulf*, London, 1953, 79.

14 A. A. HILL, *An Introduction to Linguistic Structures*, New York, 1958, which follows on the pioneering work of G. L. TRAGER and H. L. SMITH in *Studies in Linguistics*, 1951. For different, but widely accepted, notations see C. F. HOCKETT, *A Course in Modern Linguistics*, New York, 1958, Chap. 6: H. A. GLEASON, *An Introduction to Descriptive Linguistics*, New York, 1961, 167–8.

Appendix A

Since figures and percentages have been cited, the statistical basis for any such calculation must be valid. Several studies have been published, showing the proportionate use (e.g.) of Germanic, Romance, and Classical words in an author. Any examination of an author's vocabulary which merely totals his vocabulary from one source and compares it with his total vocabulary from another is statistically invalid, and the results have purely a curiosity value. The only statistically valid basis is a count of *occurrences*. Every word, no matter how frequently it recurs, must be scored. If this appears to give (as indeed it does) a high score to the constantly recurring structural Germanic words, it represents the actuality of the situation. Any literary researcher who is not prepared to accept statistical method, for whom simple arithmetic seems good enough, is driven inescapably into an engaging fallacy. If he counts 'the' and 'that' and 'when' and the rest of the recurring words as one word each and the classical words like 'inquisiturient' and 'fugitive' also as one word each, totals each group and then calculates his percentages, he will find – if he takes the trouble – that the percentage of classical words in Milton's prose grows inexorably the more pages he reads: which is absurd. In mathematical terms, the percentage he produces is a function of the size of the sample. For a full discussion of the fallacy involved, see G. U. Yule, *The Statistical Study of Literary Vocabulary*, 1944, chapter v.

Chapter 3
Continuity II: Sentence-structure

The final continuing feature of English prose is sentence-structure. It is a commonplace to observe that the meaning of a modern English sentence depends on word-order – disrupt the order and ambiguity or nonsense immediately ensues – whereas a fully inflected language like Latin permits a relatively free choice of word order. Latin verse permits even greater freedom than prose: Ovid can write 'Nec amara Tibullo tempus amicitiae fata dedere meae' – 'Nor did bitter fate grant the time for my friendship with Tibullus', where object precedes subject, the qualifying adjectives are both separated from their companion nouns, one adjective precedes its noun, the other follows it, and the verb occupies a position unlikely in Latin prose. Yet the firm links of concord in gender, number and case leave no opportunity for ambiguity.

Old English was like Latin an inflected language with similar concords. In theory, something like the same freedom should have been possible. In fact, it did not have this freedom. The movement towards a relatively fixed (and sometimes rigid) word order both in prose and in verse was well established in the earliest extant documents, and even in the still earlier Runic inscriptions. Certain of the most-used sentence-structures of modern English go back as far as the English language can be traced. This does not gainsay the subsequent enrichment and embellishment of sentence-structure that followed from the study of French and Latin and mediaeval and renaissance rhetoric. But as with vocabulary, so with the sentence. The structures embedded in word-order, the bones of the language, make their appearance early.

Here is a sentence from the late tenth-century prose of Aelfric:

> þes foresæda halga wer wæs gewunod þæt he wolde gan on niht to sæ ond standan on þam sealtan brymme oþ his swyran, singende his gebedu

literally

> This aforesaid holy man was wont that he would go at night to the sea and stand in the salt water up to his neck, chanting his prayers.

The Old English contains one idiom discarded in modern English, which today would have 'wont (or accustomed) to go'. But apart from that, the remarkable thing about the sentence is precisely that it is not remarkable. The word-order is the order of the present. Subject precedes predicate; prepositions occupy their modern position, the auxiliary verb immediately precedes the past participle, the final participial phrase is common modern usage, the adjectives precede the nouns, and they precede them in a hierarchy of proximity that follows precise rules still valid in contemporary writing.

If we examine the principal clause of almost any Old English sentence, we find there firmly established what has turned out to be the dominant sentence-structure of English. It is the subject-predicate sentence (what Bloomfield calls the actor-action sentence[1]) with a rigid subject-verb-object (svo) order. This order is so regular that extensive illustration is unnecessary. The following principal clauses from Aelfric, arranged in ascending order of complexity of modification, will show how accurately Old English word order foreshadows the word-order of the present day: *Se halga andwyrde*, 'the saint answered' (sv); *se halga ða sona andwyrde*, 'the saint then speedily answered' (sv); *se halga ða het him bringan sæd*, 'the saint then commanded to him to be brought seed' (svo); *se halga wer ða sona het þa heardnesse swiþe holian onmiddan þære flore his fægeran botles*, 'the holy man then immediately commanded the hard surface to be swiftly pierced in the middle of the floor of his fair dwelling' (svo *plus* adverbial modifier).

This is normal order, and it provides the structure of the main statement in Old English prose, and finally of all statements, principal or dependent, in later prose. It is the order of what might be called neutral narrative. The demands of rhetoric and emotion in any period of English can disrupt this normal order, bringing emphatic elements to the beginning or the end of the sentence – Blessed are the poor in spirit, say the Beatitudes; *Gode ælmiehtigum si ðonc*, 'to God almighty be thanks', writes Alfred with some emotion and a conscious reversal of normal order. But as soon as the voice drops and the narrative or the exposition continues, this sentence-structure forms the staple of all narrative sentences in English of all periods.

This establishment in Old English of a fixed order, corresponding to the order of the present day, extends beyond the svo order of principal clauses. Adjectival modifiers early settled into structural patterns which, though unrecognised until recently, are nevertheless an essential feature of the 'grammar' of modern English. There is a precise sequence of modifiers in English – one *must* say 'many holy words', 'in all fine arts', 'a very beautiful bone', 'to no other business', 'in this same year'.

No reshuffling of the order of these modifiers is possible. The contrast with Latin is again significant – 'hoc genus omne' can be written with the three words in any order without loss of meaning or idiomatic usage.

The 'rules' for the order of attributive adjectives in modern English can be determined empirically. They are fairly complex, and only a few of the main principles need be noted.[2] Briefly, adjectives of description come closest to the noun (good men); 'determining' adjectives like 'this' and 'other' precede adjectives of description (these good men; other good men); where the determiner is definite, numerating adjectives follow it (these three good men); where it is indefinite, the numerating adjective precedes it (three other good men). Where there is more than one descriptive adjective, the pattern of proximity follows strict and describable conventions (good old black men). Where there is a series of modifiers, each occupies its fixed position (all these three good old black men).

It comes with something of a shock of recognition to discover that the fixed order of adjectives is nothing new. It has been fixed for well over a thousand years. The empiric 'rules' for adjective order in present-day English are substantially the 'rules' for their order in Old English prose. The phrases given in the last paragraph but two have their precise equivalents in the Old English of Alfred, Aelfric and the *Chronicle*, from which indeed they are taken – *monig halwende word; on eallum godum cræftum; swiþe æpele ban; to nanre oðerre note; on þyssum ilcan geare.*

The Old English inflexional bonds of noun with verb and adjective with noun were thus reinforced by a rigid structural grouping. The adjective modified the noun and 'belonged' to it as much by proximity as by grammatical concord. Position as well as case identified the subject and the object. Position was probably the more important; certainly this rigid structural pattern, established so early in the language, goes a long way towards explaining how inflexions could weaken without resultant loss of meaning. It is usually assumed that a fixed word-order took over the task of the lost inflexions. The truth is more likely to be the other way round. The fixed word-order made the inflexional endings redundant. They were losing their force before the end of the Old English period.

A full comparison of word order in Old English and modern English lies outside the scope of this study; it is a task that has not yet been attempted. But one further comparison will illuminate how close Old English structure can be to that of the present day. In a narrative sentence in modern English adverbial modifiers (words or phrases) tend to occur in a fixed order. A very common sequence in written prose is time-manner-place:

> He took off his shoes and *then* (1) crept *silently* (2) *across the room* (3).
> *The previous night* (1) he had slept *peacefully* (2) *on the bed by the window* (3).

This sequence was well established in Old English, as can be seen in two sample sentences from Wulfstan and Aelfric:

> Dæghwamlice (1) man unriht rærde *ealles to wide* (2) *gynd ealle þas ðeode* (3).
> Every day they have committed injustice all too widely in all this nation.
> Se halga wer *ða sona* (1) het þa heardnesse *swiðe* (2) holian *onmiddan þære flore* (3).
> The holy man then immediately commanded the hard surface to be swiftly pierced in the middle of the floor.

Much work remains to be done on the sentence-structure of Old English. But two strong impressions emerge from a study of our early prose. They are well summed up by Quirk and Wrenn in their *Old English Grammar*, 'First, that there are in OE considerable areas of conformity to describable patterns; secondly, that these patterns to a great extent coincide with modern usage.'[3] The heavy concentration of most grammars of Old English on phonology and accidence (in which the older language differs most obviously from the modern tongue) has tended to divert attention from the considerable areas of coincidence. In its essentials the structure of the Old English sentence is the structure of today.

Differences there are, and it is interesting to watch in the period between the tenth and the fourteenth century the inexorable shaping of the modern sentence. In early writing the position of the pronoun-object ran counter to the normal svo order. Old English often put the pronoun object *before* the verb. This older order is still possible in poetry – 'Him the Almighty Power hurled headlong' is common Miltonic usage. In the late *Chronicle* (AD 1137) usage wavers – 'þe biscopes *heom* (them) cursede' appears within a few lines of 'me (i.e. they) smoked *heom* (them) mid ful smoke'. By the fourteenth century the order is that of today. It is possible that one of the factors that assisted the change, bringing pronoun-order in line with noun-order, was the development of accusative forms for the pronoun with the full phonetic weight of monosyllabic nouns. Some of the Old English pronoun-object forms, notable the overworked 'hie' (which had

to do duty for 'she', 'her', 'they', and 'them') were phonetically 'light'
They could barely carry the stress expected of a noun in the object
position. When the phonetically 'heavier' forms 'her' and 'them' were
developed, alongside the emphatic monosyllables 'him' and 'it' and the
older 'me', 'thee' and 'you', English had acquired a full series of pronoun-
objects that could carry the required stress for the object position, and
from late Middle English the pronouns conform to the normal svo
sentence order.

One common Old English sentence-structure, often met in the *Chronicle*,
was early discarded in narrative prose. This was the sentence that begins
with a demonstrative word like *þa* 'then' or *her* 'Here, at this point in the
narrative'. In such sentences the order is verb-subject (vs) or verb-subject-
object (vso) – 'Her for se here' – 'at this point advanced the raiding army'
(vs); 'þa besæt sio fierd hie' – 'then besieged the army them' (vso).
Although this order vanished from narrative prose, as later writers grew
more skilful at subordination of clauses, it has remained alive in more
elevated contexts – the 'here lies' of the epitaph, and the 'then shall the
curate', 'then shall the Bishop' of the Prayer Book. Keats, with his sure
instinct for the language, relies on it for subtle reinforcement in his line:
'Then felt I like some watcher of the skies.'

The svo structure of the principal clause became the structure for all
clauses. The process took some time. Old English dependent clauses tend
to have their object before the verb (sov). A sentence from Ælfric shows
two instances:

> Cuþbertus þam folce fægere bodade, þæt hi *wære* wæron wið
> deofles syrwan, þylæsðe he mid leasunge heora *geleafan* awyrde
>
> *literally*
> Cuthbert to the people fairly preached, that they *wary* be against
> the devil's snares, lest he with deceit their *faith* corrupt.

The displacement, to modern ears, of the complement 'wære' – 'wary'
and the object 'geleafan' – 'faith' remained a feature of Old English prose
down to the late *Chronicle*, where we can often find constructions like:
'þa the suikes undergaeton ðat he *milde man* was' – 'when the traitors
discovered that he a *gentle man* was.'

In the thirteenth century, the svo order of the principal clause finally
asserted its dominance and it became the standard pattern for clauses of all
types. The modern practice – normal order in both principal and dependent clauses except for deliberate rhetorical inversions – can be seen beginning in R. W. Chambers' twelfth-century touchstone of continuity, the

Ancrene Riwle. By the fourteenth century we read a sentence like Rolle of Hampole's 'Bot thou sall witt þat no man hase *perfite syght of heven*' or Chaucer's 'I prey meekly every discreet persone that redeth or hereth *this litel tretis*' and recognise the completely modern shape of the sentence. A further area of coincidence has been established.

This discussion has been confined to the clauses as isolated units. They are the bricks from which the sentence is built. The bricks have changed little over the years, though ways of building have altered. Such alterations belong to subsequent chapters, but a brief glance ahead will show that even in the midst of development the instinct for continuity is remarkably persistent. Modern English differs most sharply from Old English in the greater flexibility and subtlety with which it can link clauses together. It has resources for expressing relationship in varying levels of subordination unknown to the earlier tongue. In general, however, the process of development has been addition without much subtraction. English learned new devices without giving up the old.

Two of the commonest methods used in Old English for linking clauses are co-ordination and parataxis. In co-ordination, the sentence consists of a series of main statements joined by 'and' or a comparable linking-word:

Ic   arise, *ond* ic fare to minum fæder, *ond*   ic secge him.
I will arise, *and*   go to my   father, *and*   will say unto him.

In parataxis, the linking-words are absent. The main statements are set down side by side. In place of the linking-word, there was in speech a firm pause or juncture:

Drihten, hæle us; we mote forwurþan.
Lord,   save us: we perish.

This kind of structure is generally called 'primitive'.[4] The term is hardly accurate, if primitive carries its normal connotation of something rudimentary and archaic which is discarded by an advancing culture. English discarded neither type of sentence-structure, and the Old English procedures of writing principal clauses joined by 'ands' and 'buts' and of paratactic construction, buttressed if need be by the most obvious and unsophisticated dependent clauses, have remained permanent features of good prose, and not merely the good prose of 'simple' writers.

A few examples will suffice. Milton, expert though he is in the complicated periodic sentence of later times, frequently writes with telling effect sentences of pure Old English structure:

And yet on the other hand unless wariness be used, as good almost kill

> a Man as kill a good Book; who kills a Man kills a reasonable creature, God's Image; but he who destroys a good Book, kills reason itself, kills the Image of God, as it were in the eye.

Alfred's vocabulary did not include 'reason', 'image', 'destroy', or 'creature', but he would have given this sentence exactly the same shape. Much of the essentially conservative prose of the Authorised Version is based on the Old English uncomplicated co-ordination and parataxis of clauses:

> And his disciples came to him, and awoke him, saying, Lord, save us: we perish.

A century later Defoe can write an effective paratactic series:

> I stood like one thunderstruck, or as if I had seen an apparition: I listened, I looked around me, I could hear nothing, nor see anything. I went up to a rising ground to look further; I could see no other impression but that one.

Across two further centuries Virginia Woolf can turn aside from the complexities of interior monologue to echo the same movement:

> She held up her hand. She stopped the cab opposite a little row of posts in an alley. She got out and made her way into the Square.

In language, as in other things, England discards little of its past.

We can now look back at the material presented in the opening three chapters and reassess the question of continuity. After the publication of Chambers' study, it was generally accepted that Old English, not the Renaissance, should be regarded as the real starting-point. English prose of every period is continuously illuminated and explained in the light of what has gone before. Innovations are always possible, and cannot be ignored, but they never form more than a minority element in the usage of any particular time. New elements have been constantly introduced: in every period, enrichment of the vocabulary from foreign sources; in the Renaissance, a longer and more complex sentence-structure modelled on classical Latin; in Middle English, French influence on the construction of phrases and sometimes of sentences. In recent years doubts have been cast on the Chambers thesis: a revival of interest in the links between English and French has led some writers (notably Norman Davis,[5] the editor of the Paston Letters) to suggest that French influence was so pervasive in the late mediaeval period that the concept of continuity is untenable.

But continuity there was, and it rests on a basis broader than Chambers proposed. It does not depend simply on the preservation of Alfredian prose in manuscripts of Middle English homilies. Continuity is the result of the only way in which language is transmitted, by a kind of oral indoctrination. Man learns to speak from man, not from books. His speech habits are formed long before he learns to read. This has meant that the basic structures of English have changed very little, and if a foreign element (introduced from French or elsewhere) is to be viable, it must conform rapidly to English speech habits. The segmented English sentence, stressed in word-groups, each word-group separated from its neighbour by a boundary-marker, the major stress of each group falling on the semantically important word in the group, the groups occurring in a relatively fixed order, the words in each group generally falling in a precisely fixed order – all this, plus the continuity of the original vocabulary and the preservation of the original structural words, has ensured an underlying stability in English speech, and in the prose which is based upon it.

Granted this stability, the English language has been able to take innovation from other languages in its stride. Foreign words, re-sounded with native phonemes and assimilated to the native stress-system, have been easily adopted, and generally retained. Non-native structural patterns (as later chapters will show in more detail) have not so readily won a place. The late seventeenth century ruthlessly discarded the structural innovations of the renaissance humanists: the French-shaped clausal links of fourteenth- and fifteenth-century prose gained no permanent foothold in the language; most of Chaucer's Gallicisms (like 'al-outerly', patterned on *tout outrement*) were quietly dropped in the century following his death. Prins and Orr have collected many hundreds of 'French-based' English phrases from several centuries of English usage.[6] An examination of these suggests that in order to be a candidate for retention (as *tenir sa langue* has been retained in 'hold one's tongue') the foreign phrase must on its introduction be itself structured as if it were already English. The English language has retained numerous extraneous elements, but only – because of the continuous pressure exerted by speech – in terms of its own phonemic, stress, and structural system.

So long as these innovations do not break the mould of English expression, they can be a source of enrichment. But if the exotic influence becomes dominant (particularly if the eye on the printed page rather than the sensitive ear is the guide), danger is at hand, and a shift towards a speech-base seems inevitable. Such a reaction occurred at the end of the seventeenth century, when the 'digressions and swellings' of mid-century were abandoned by the Royal Society in favour of a 'close, naked, natural way of speaking'. The revolution of the late seventeenth century is only one, generally the best documented, of a series of adjustments (to be considered in later chapters) each of which ensured that English prose did not deviate too far from what it is difficult to call other than a continuity of the native line.

Notes

1 L. BLOOMFIELD, *Language*, New York, 1950, 172–7.
2 cf. BLOOMFIELD, pp. 202–6; A. A. HILL, *Introduction to Linguistic Structures*, New York, 1958, 175–90.
3 R. QUIRK, & C. L. WRENN, *An Old English Grammar*, London, 1958, 87.
4 A. H. SMITH, *The Parker Chronicle*, London, 1935, 15.
5 N. DAVIS, 'Styles in English Prose', *Actes du 8e Congrès de la Fédération Internationale des Langues et Littératures Modernes*, Liège, 1961. The influence of French on English was studied by E. EINENKEL in vol. i. of Paul's Grundriss; cf. also S. POTTER 'Gallicisms Past and Present' in *Essays and Studies*, 15, 1962.
6 A. A. PRINS, *French Influence on English Phrasing*, Leiden, 1952; J. ORR, *The Impact of French upon English*, Oxford, 1948; J. ORR, *Old French and Modern English Idiom*, Oxford, 1962.

Part two The Middle Ages

Chapter 4

The Varieties of Anglo-Saxon Prose

The prose of the Old English period is for most readers disappointing. They can admit the value of what it contains for the study of history or law or archaeology. But apart from the occasional moving passage its literary merits seem dubious. Compared with the elegiac poetry of *The Wanderer* or *The Ruin* or the heroic tone of *Maldon* or *Beowulf*, its effects seem pedestrian and flat. Such disappointment is understandable in readers with literary expectations. But it arises from a misconception, a presumption that poetry and prose – particularly at this early stage – should be doing the same job. The audience for Old English poetry expected that its recital would give them pleasure. *Beowulf*, in the words of Dorothy Whitelock, is 'first and foremost literature of entertainment'.[1] The 'consumer' of Old English prose, on the other hand, did not expect entertainment from what he read or heard. He expected to be informed and instructed. Old English prose is basically a prose of utility.

Unless he accepts this basis, the reader of Old English prose is continually looking for the wrong things. He passes impatiently over the 'dull' factual passages, looking forward to the exciting piece of narration or the revealing personal touch or the emotional appeal. He is unconsciously applying criteria which do not have relevance until several centuries later in the development of English prose. It was never the intention of the writer of Old English prose to produce a series of pieces that could be admired in a later anthology.

If we accept Old English prose for what it was, a prose of utility, it is possible to judge it accordingly, and to find an extremely effective medium of communication capable, for example, of recording facts and events and observations accurately and economically, capable of enunciating a legal system and the intricacies of land tenure and transfer without ambiguity, a vernacular medium (in an age when the educated spoke and wrote in Latin) of notable efficiency for elementary and adult education and for exhortation from the pulpit. Such a prose may be simple; it would be a mistake to regard it as primitive.[2] It performed its functions admirably;

and it was to be the basis for the much more complex and literary usages that later centuries were to demand.

Prose of Exposition

One of the essential jobs of Old English prose was the communication of instructions. Three important groups of manuscripts have survived recording prose of this type, namely medical and 'scientific' manuscripts, the corpus of Anglo-Saxon law, and the extant manuscripts of Anglo-Saxon wills and charters. None of the writers of this type of material show any signs of the study of the literary devices of mediaeval rhetoric; they are concerned solely with the problem of accurate communication; for this they use a language and a sentence-structure derived directly from the speech of their times.

The three volumes of Cockayne's *Leechdoms* afford many examples of prose which though simple and colloquial conveys its instructions with accuracy and economy;

> þeos wyrt þe man betonicam nemneð heo biþ cenned on mædum ond on clænum dunlandum ond on gefriþedum stowum. Seo deah gehwæþer ge þæs mannes sawle ge his lichoman. Hio hine scyldeþ wið unhyrum nihtgengum ond wiþ egeslicum gesihðum ond swefnum; ond seo wyrt byþ swiþe haligu; ond þus þu hi scealt niman on agustes monþe butan iserne; ond þonne þu hi genumene hæbbe, ahryse þa moldan of, þæt hyre nanwiht on ne clifie, ond þonne drig hi on sceade swiþe þearle, ond mid wyrttruman mid ealle gewyrc to duste. Bruc hyre þonne, and hyre byrig þonne þu bedurfe.[3]

> This plant which is called betony grows in meadows and clean downlands and in shady places. It is good both for man's soul and for his body. It protects him against monstrous night-visitors and dreadful visions and dreams; and the plant is very wholesome; and thus must you gather it – in the month of August without iron tool; and when you have gathered it, shake the earth off, till nothing clings on it, and dry it in the shade thoroughly, and (roots and all) pound it to dust. Use it then, and taste of it when you need.

Allied to this instructional style, with its avoidance of subordinate clauses, is the style of the early Anglo-Saxon laws. In its simplest form, the Anglo-Saxon law consists of two clauses, a condition and a penalty:

Gif ðeowmon wyrce on Sunnandæg be his hlafordes hæse, sie he
frioh ...

If a slave works on Sunday by his lord's command, he shall become
free ...

On occasion there may be added an explanatory clause:

þonne man beam on wuda forbærne, ond weorðe yppe on þone ðe
hit dyde, gielde fulwite; geselle LX scillinga forþamþe fyr bið þeof.[4]

If anyone burns up a tree in the wood, and it becomes evident who
did it, he shall pay a full fine; he shall pay 60 shillings, because fire is
a thief.

Few of the early laws show more complicated syntax than this.

Anglo-Saxon wills are of particular importance for a study of early
prose. They are perhaps the closest we can come to the actual spoken
English of the period. The Anglo-Saxon will was not a 'legal' document
in the modern sense. Following the Germanic custom, the man preparing
for death spoke his words in the presence of witnesses; he 'spoke his *cwide*
(speech)'. This completed the formality. The writing was merely the
documentation of the oral will.[5] Wills, therefore (the best known is
Alfred's own), are excellent examples of prose of instruction at its most
colloquial, and the surviving wills dispose efficiently of estates, swords,
gold cups, bullocks, and other chattels to the appropriate legatee with the
minimum of fuss.

Somewhat more formal (because in this case the actual document was
valuable) are the Anglo-Saxon charters. They tend to have more flourish
at the beginning and the end, mainly owing to the influence of the Latin
formulae from which they derive:

In Godes name ich Aþelstan   God gyuing   king welding eal
Brytone · mid alle mine witene · ond alle biscope of kinedome of
Engelonde · gelad by þe priccinge of ðe Haly Goste · grante and
confirmye by ðisse minre chartre ...[6]

In the name of God, I, Aethelstan, by the grace of God King ruling
the whole of Britain, along with all my councillors and all the bishops
of the kingdom of England, led by the spurring of the Holy Ghost,
grant and confirm by this my charter ...

But once into the body of the text, the charters relapse to the direct and uncomplicated norm of Anglo-Saxon prose of instruction.

The surviving writings of Aelfric indicate that the use of such a style was the result not of ineptitude but of deliberate choice. Aelfric could write with a considerable degree of complexity, conscious rhythm, and rhetorical sophistication when the occasion demanded. But his three educational treatises, his work on astronomy the *De Temporibus Anni*, his school textbook the *Colloquy*, and particularly his *Grammar* preserve the unemphatic tone and simple sentence-structure of Anglo-Saxon instructional prose:

> Littera is stæf on Englisc and is se læsta dæl on bocum and unto-daeledlic. We todælað þa boc to cwydum, and syððan ða cwydas to daelum, eft ða dælas to stæfgefegum, and syððan þa stæfgefegu to stafum.[7]

> *Littera* is 'letter' in English and is the smallest element in a piece of writing and is indivisible. We divide a piece of writing into sentences, and then the sentences into words, then the words into syllables, and the syllables into letters.

Ælfric clearly considered that this was the appropriate style for the matter in hand.

With this unrhetorical and purely functional prose of exposition, we are close to the movement of actual speech. It is the language of instructions and of instruction; it is the language of the King's – and other men's – business and can be heard in the extant Anglo-Saxon writs in which their commands were conveyed; it is also the language of the early entries in the *Anglo-Saxon Chronicle* and of the West Saxon Gospels; an unglamorised plain speech of main statements and few subordinate clauses that is yet capable of conveying complicated technicalities. On its foundations were built the other varieties of Anglo-Saxon prose – the more fluid progression of Alfred, the graceful narrative of Aelfric, and even the latter-day fulminations of Wulfstan. In later centuries *The Master of Game*, *Toxophilus*, *The Compleat Angler*, *The Skeptical Chymist*, and *Directions to Servants* continue to demonstrate its permanence in the fabric of English prose.

Alfred and the Prose of Adult Education

Alfred's extensive writings occupy a central position in the development of English prose. They are an outgrowth from the language of instruction.

Apart from a few passages of personal expansion (some of them of extreme importance) his work was all translated or adapted from Latin. His reasons for writing were given in the well-known preface to his translation of Pope Gregory's *Cura Pastoralis*: in the latter part of his reign, the Danes defeated but the country ravaged and education at a low ebb, he decided to translate important Latin books into English so that all free-born youths might have text-books in English. His further hope was that the most ambitious of them would then master Latin. In the space of a few years he produced Anglo-Saxon versions of a whole series of further mediaeval educational texts: Boethius's *Consolations of Philosophy*; Orosius's *Compendious History of the World*; the *Soliloquies* of St. Augustine; and he had some hand in a version of Bede's *Ecclesiastical History of the English People*.

Alfred's English style is based on Anglo-Saxon instructional prose. But he creates from it what is virtually a new medium. He was not writing medical prescriptions for leeches or a grammar for young pupils, but texts for young men who already had a colloquial command of their own tongue. He had ever in front of him his mediaeval Latin originals, not classical Latin, but nevertheless Latin of a syntactical density unknown in Anglo-Saxon instructional prose. Finally his own personality often breaks through; his reading, his knowledge of Old English poetry and of rhetoric, and the sheer intensity of his educational campaign add colour, metaphor, and poetic turns of expression to many passages of his prose. Alfred has left us some 'anthology pieces', but not – significantly – in the main body of his educational writings.

What is remarkable about his writing, indeed, is the independent way in which he adapts the Latin. He translates – as he says himself 'hwilum word be worde, hwilum ondgit of andgite' – 'sometimes word by word, sometimes following the general sense of the passage' – but he translates into English, not into Latinised Anglo-Saxon. He is unaffected by Latin word-order, rendering unerringly into the natural word-order of English, and he breaks up without compunction the Latin periodic sentence into a series of characteristic English type clauses, often in parataxis, each one adding in succession a further expansion of meaning.

A short sentence from Boethius[8] will illustrate his command of English idiom. How does one translate the following? '*Quibus in ipsis inest ratio, inest etiam volendi nolendique libertas*', *literally* 'For those whom in themselves there exists reason, there exists the freedom of willing or refusing.' This is a mere construe, not a translation. Alfred never construes. He passes the Latin through his mind and rejects constructions (like *volendi libertas*) that are alien to his English. What emerges is a four-clause sentence which preserves the sense of the Latin but rejects its syntax. The result, with its successive additions, moves in the rhythm of spoken English:

> Aelc mon hæfð þone freodom þæt he wat hwæt he wile, hwæt he nele.
>
> Each man has the freedom that he knows what he wills, what he does not will.

The major stresses fall on the emphatic words, 'freodom', 'wat', 'wile', 'nele'. The junctures are the junctures of English speech. The abstractions of the Latin are replaced by concrete imagery (*quibus* becoming 'each *man*'), and the gerunds by active finite verbs.

Concrete imagery and the active verb are, indeed, general characteristics of Alfred's prose. Two striking examples are the preface – which is independent writing not translation – to his version of St. Augustine's *Soliloquies*, where the imagery is all derived from the timbering of a house, and secondly the adaptation of a simile in Boethius, where Boethius uses the image of a group of 'orbs' circling one centre, almost certainly derived from Ptolemaic astronomy. Alfred's image is a waggon wheel turning on its axle, and the simile worked out in considerable detail is much more forceful and clearer than the Latin original. Independent additions elsewhere – notably the Ohthere and Wulfstan accounts of northern voyages inserted into his *Orosius* – have the same concrete quality.

The claim is not exaggerated that Alfred is the father of English prose. The prose of instruction on which he based his style could be only limited in its application. Alfred, while keeping its basic movement, expanded its scope and lengthened its sentence and probably (though it is more difficult here to be sure) enriched its vocabulary. He acquired (it was in his Latin originals) a sense of paragraph construction. He made of English an efficient medium through which much of the learning of mediaeval Europe could be transmitted to Englishmen of the ninth century and later.

Alfred's part in the *Anglo-Saxon Chronicle* cannot be demonstrated directly. In ninth-century Wessex a chronicle was gathered together from various sources probably under Alfred's influence. The early entries are generally bare, in the baldest 'utility' style. During Alfred's reign the entries grow longer, and though the sentence-structure remains relatively simple, the whole writing shows a narrative skill and a forward impetus that is new to Anglo-Saxon. The chronicle project was kept going in various centres for some time after Alfred's death, in one instance (the Peterborough manuscript) until the middle of the twelfth century. It thus presents a continuous document of the development of what can fairly be called Alfredian prose as far as early Middle English, a sober prose of record that can on occasion be extremely moving.

Prose of Persuasion

If the teacher is responsible for the first development of English prose, the second development belonged to the preacher. A considerable number of homilies and sermons survive. Only two names, Aelfric and Wulfstan, need concern us. The prose of both differs considerably from the prose of Alfred. But it is still a prose of utility. The two writers, even when they elaborate the movement of earlier prose, adding new rhythms for oral delivery, keep their minds and their prose style firmly directed to a practical end. There are no words merely for the words' sake. Anglo-Saxon religious prose is prose of persuasion, and the rhetorical devices are there to produce an effect on a congregation.

Alfred had been an educated layman. Aelfric and Wulfstan were learned clerics, and this meant that they carried into their conception of writing the full teaching of mediaeval rhetoric, particularly as expounded and analysed in Augustine's *De Doctrina Christiana*. Behind Augustine lay Cicero's *De Oratore* and after Augustine came mediaeval summaries of his teaching. On the basis of these texts, mediaeval rhetoric recognised three functions of writing – *docere, delectare, movere*, teaching, giving pleasure, and moving the emotions – and three corresponding styles, *tenue, medium,* and *grande*, the plain, the middle, and the elevated.[9] Wulfstan did not favour the plain teaching style. Aelfric (as has been noted) used it in his educational textbooks.

For both writers, the major job was to persuade. Aelfric was prepared to include *delectare*, the giving of pleasure, when the occasion suited (as it did in some of his narratives). Wulfstan restricted himself to *movere*, arousing terror and repentance in his listeners.

The problem for both was to find a way of writing (and preaching) in Anglo-Saxon which could correspond to the *grande* or elevated style in Latin. The Latin periodic sentence was beyond them. The nature of the English sentence-construction of their time made it impossible to imitate the interlocking of Latin clauses. Both struck on a device for elaborating their prose on the basis of Germanic rhythm. Anglo-Saxon poetry had for several centuries settled into the formalised two-stress half-line; Anglo-Saxon 'Alfredian' prose had accepted the regular (but not formalised) stresses of ordinary conversation. Somewhere between these two a new prose style could be created which could be *grande*, or elevated.

In Aelfric's writings the process can be seen developing. His 'personal' writing (for example, the preface to his *Homilies*) is essentially Alfredian prose. His sentence is generally longer than Alfred's, he is clearly more of a professional in his handling of words and constructions, but his style is close to the conversational norm. In his earliest groups of religious writings (his *Homilies*, c. AD 990) alliteration and a more insistent rhythm are constantly present. In his later *Lives of Saints* (c. AD 998) he writes in formally stressed prose 'lines'. Each prose line breaks into two half-lines. The series of strong stresses makes each line and half-line a recognisable unit. Alliteration is frequent, though not to the extent demanded by poetry:

> Hwæt ða Martianus   se manfulla cwellere
> hæfde langsum gewinn   wið þone æðelan Iulianum,

> Lo then Martianus   the evil tormentor
> Had a long struggle   with the noble Julianus.

This is the 'elevated' preaching style of Aelfric. It is not Anglo-Saxon poetry, but it is equally not the prose of conversation or simple narrative. The insistent rhythm and the regular prose-line unit must have produced an effect analogous to chanting, a formal prose written for the ear and not the eye. Aelfric's 'elevation' was confined to rhythmical devices. Even in his most elaborately conceived homilies his vocabulary remained at a normal prose level. He intended to move his hearers, but not at the expense of understanding.

With Wulfstan the process of formalised rhythm proceeds further. His homilies were delivered in a series of two-stressed phrases, each one a separate syntactical unit:[10]

> Ac wæs hére ond húnger
> brýne ond blódgyte
> on gewelhwýlcan énde
> óft ond gelóme.

> But there have been raids and starvation
> burning and bloodshed
> in nearly every quarter
> often and often.

The stressing is reinforced by alliteration and the pairing of words (often rhyming), by long cumulative lists (e.g. of sins or of penalties) and by considerable repetition. Wulfstan hammered home his injunctions as Carlyle (a kindred spirit) was to do many centuries later. Like Aelfric, he avoided poetic vocabulary and poetic figures of speech – in terms of mediaeval rhetoric, his figures (epanaphora, homoioteleuteia, the 'like beginnings' and 'like endings' of later rhetoric and the rest) are figures of 'sound' and not of 'thought'. His elaboration, his *grande* style, depends on his repetitions and his formalised rhythm, not on any incandescence of language. Oddly enough, it is Alfred, the writer of work-a-day prose, not the cleric, who can add a glow with a metaphor or a simile.

By the time of the Conquest the two major Old English styles – the prose of utility and the rhythmic prose of persuasion – were firmly established. The first remained. The second finally disappeared. Wulfstan's sermons continued to be preached in the West after his death. They were read into the twelfth century. But while preaching in the vernacular *ad populum* (to be distinguished from preaching in Latin *ad clerum*) continued in the Middle English period, there are few surviving examples of elevated rhythmical prose later than the eleventh century. The absence of manuscripts may be due to accident. But it is unlikely. The numerous surviving manuscripts of Middle English homilies written in an intimate and colloquial style points clearly to a change in taste. There was, it must be confessed, a heavy monotony in the rhythmic style of preaching. It turned out to be for English a development with no future. The true elevated style for English lay in a different kind of elaboration. It was not to come till Englishmen by-passed the theory of *De Oratore* and went to Cicero's actual speeches.

With the Conquest, the discontinuance for two centuries of the official use of English meant for the time being the end of any real motive for elaborate public English prose. It did not mean the end of religious writing. But the characteristic religious prose of the early Middle English period is designed for personal instruction or for reading in a religious community rather than for pulpit oratory. Here Alfredian prose continued, close as ever to the norm of everyday life. It was to remain the staple for the next few hundred years.

The final achievement of Anglo-Saxon prose was considerable. It became a flexible and apt medium for what it set out to express, the only European vernacular capable of handling the philosophy, the science and the theology of the time, creating from its own resources the needed abstract vocabulary. By the year 1000 (in the words of Kemp Malone) 'this newcomer could measure swords with Latin in every department of expression, and was incomparably superior to the French speech that came in with William of Normandy'.[11]

Notes

1   D. WHITELOCK, *The Audience of Beowulf*, Oxford, 1952, 20.
2   'Primitive': A. H. SMITH, ed., *The Parker Chronicle*, London, 1957, 15; 'very elementary': E. E. WARDALE, *Chapters in Old English Literature*, London, 1935, 238.
3   O. COCKAYNE, ed., *Leechdoms, Wortcunnings, and Starcraft of Early England*, London, 1864 (reprint 1961), i, 70.
4   F. L. ATTENBOROUGH, ed., *The Laws of the Early English Kings*, Cambridge, 1922, 36; 50.
5   D. WHITELOCK, ed., *Anglo-Saxon Wills*, Cambridge, 1930: General Preface by H. D. HAZELTINE, viii–xv.
6   A. J. ROBERTSON, *Anglo-Saxon Charters*, Cambridge, 1939, 44.
7   R. KAISER, *Medieval English*, Berlin, 1961, 145, 'Aelfric's Grammar'.
8   BOETHIUS, *The Consolations of Philosophy*, iv, prose 6.
9   C. S. BALDWIN, *Ancient Rhetoric and Poetic*, Gloucester, Mass., 1928, 56ff.
10 A. MCINTOSH, 'Wulfstan's Prose', *Proceedings of the British Academy*, 35, 1949, 114–16.
11 A. C. BAUGH, ed., *A Literary History of England*, New York, 1948, 10.

Chapter 5
Middle English

The period from the eleventh to the end of the fourteenth century saw the evolution of an English which in vocabulary and even (by the end of the period) in spelling is recognisable by a modern reader. Chaucer, *Piers Plowman*, and the writings of the Gawain-poet conclude the fourteenth century with a flowering of great poetry. Prose during these centuries has had less record in the literary histories, which have tended to ignore Middle English prose and to regard Malory in the fifteenth century and the Authorised Version a century and a half later as 'miracles', incapable of any explanation in terms of what has gone before. Middle English prose finds, for many readers (and alas, many non-readers), a suitable repository in the dull-brown volumes of the Early English Text Society, formidable nineteenth-century-type editions with considerable introductions on dialectal phonology.

The position of English in the period was not such as to encourage what most modern readers would regard as prose literature. After the Conquest a French-speaking minority took possession. The Court, the great landowners, and the higher clergy were French and spoke their own tongue, with Latin as the medium of the educated. English was left to the mass of the people and the lower clergy. It was neither discouraged nor encouraged. It was simply not used in official circles. The small group of English landowners who retained their estates and their titles aligned themselves socially and linguistically with the newcomers. A literature came into being for the new patrons. Inevitably, it was written in French – in Anglo-Norman to be more precise. It was almost exclusively verse: saints' lives, romances, lays, lyrics and fabliaus.

A century and a half after the Conquest, it would be too much to claim that the French were absorbed. But they were no longer Normans. The loss of Normandy in 1204, and the decrees of the Kings of England and of France of 1244, which made it illegal to hold land in both countries, began, even at the moment of its greatest literary triumphs, the decline of Anglo-Norman as the official tongue. During the remainder of the thirteenth century English became increasingly the language of the upper as well as of the lower class, and by 1300 its use was for most practical purposes accepted. Throughout the fourteenth century both personal references and public records make it clear that this ascendency was being officially recognised: a decree of the University of Oxford of 1322 (which can be paralleled elsewhere in the century) insisted that only Latin or French be used in conversation, a sure sign that English was a common medium; in 1362 English was made the language of pleading in the courts of law. This fourteenth-century change from French to English is underlined (and pin-pointed in date) in Trevisa's translation of Higden's 'world-history', the *Polychronicon*. Higden writing in Latin about 1330 noted that in England French was the language of children's education. Trevisa, writing an English translation in 1385, is impelled to add a note that the situation has 'somdel ychaunged': in all the grammar schools of England children are taught in English and as a result 'conneþ no more Frensch þan can here lift heele.' French, by the end of the fourteenth century, had become a language of polite accomplishment, no longer a medium of general or official communication.

Nevertheless, its influence on English authors remained powerful, and this apart from the obvious increase in vocabulary borrowing. The fashion-able kinds of writing remain French in form. The class which had listened to Anglo-Norman lays and romances in the thirteenth century did not change their taste when they changed their language. The verse romance, the rhyming chronicle, the fable, the lay, the dream allegory, and the lyric written in English continued to provide the same kind of reading (or listening) for the same kind of society. Verse, not prose, was what they looked for, and what they received. Even when some of the elements of the French influence were not adopted by the writers (as in the poetry of the fourteenth-century alliterative revival) the ultimate outcome is still verse. Chaucer, the practised professional at the end of the period, wrote the genres that his courtly audience expected.

What happened to prose and prose-writing during the time? If, as has been argued in the first chapter, English prose did not die, who kept it alive? The answer is twofold. The majority of the population kept it alive by continuing to speak it. The Church kept it alive as the medium of in-struction, in sermons and homilies and manuals of conduct. This was not a worldly-fashionable way of writing but it was a task of intense serious-ness. The parish-priest, charged with the cure of souls,

þat han cure under Criste and crouning in tokne,

dealt almost exclusively with men and women who knew nothing but their native English. If they were to be instructed, English was the only medium. And if the priest was negligent or ill-equipped, he soon found formidable opposition from the Dominican and the Franciscan friars who arrived in England, to preach, in the early thirteenth century. The friars lengthened the sermon at the expense of the mass and made great use of the 'exemplum' – the inset short story – often with considerable narrative skill. Under the Franciscan Archbishop of Canterbury, John Peckham, a general council issued in 1281 the Constitutions of Lambeth, by which it became mandatory for all priests to preach on the main points of the faith four times a year, in English.[1] The Middle English sermon *ad populum* so continued throughout the period the blend of instruction and narrative that had found its best earlier expression in the homilies of Aelfric. Many have survived in manuscript.

One special group attracted the attention of religious writers: the women who retreated to nunneries. It would be quite false to think of them as uneducated. Many came from noble houses and brought to the nunnery the secular culture of their class (Chaucer's prioress is above all a *lady*). But they did not know, and were not expected to know, Latin. The rules of their order, the lives of the women saints on whom they could fasten their thoughts, the material for their meditation and even for their entertainment, all had to be in English and in prose, the natural medium of the Church. Unquestionably the best prose of the period was written for this cultured and appreciative group. It was not to be the last time that an audience of women would have a telling effect on English prose.

'Anglo-Saxon' (or 'Old English') and 'Middle English' are labels of relatively recent scholarship. They define linguistic periods which, from the perspective of the nineteenth and the twentieth centuries, are clearly different. But there was, of course, no abrupt transition or sudden change. Old English of the classical type continued to be used until at least the end of the eleventh century – many of our important OE texts are derived from post-Conquest manuscripts. The *Chronicle* continued. The laws remained in Anglo-Saxon for a time but were inevitably an early casualty, giving way to Latin before 1100. Religious writing continued as if the Conquest had never taken place, using the sentence patterns of the older language, even though the pronunciation (and terminations) of the individual words underwent considerable modification.

Yet, once into the Middle English period, the modern reader is conscious of a different linguistic situation. The four dialects of Old English were not so very far apart, and the pre-eminence of Wessex had over much of the Old English period established Alfred's West Saxon speech as literally 'the King's English'. During the centuries of Anglo-Norman domination there was no such accepted 'central' English. The dialects diverged further till East differed sharply from West and the Northener (from York, not distant Scotland) spoke to the Southerner a 'strange wlaffyng, chyteryng, harryng and garryng, grisbittyng'. In the manuscript (with every man spelling his own dialect his own way) and on the printed page, Middle English looks like a transcript of Babel.

But behind all this linguistic diversity lies a basic unity. The differences are in the phonology, not in the syntax. The Anglo-Saxon sentence patterns continue. For this reason in this chapter many of the Middle English passages cited will be modernised in spelling. If writers use the same sentence pattern, it is immaterial for this study whether they called a 'sin' a 'sunne' or 'sinne' or 'zenne', whether they wrote 'each' as 'uche' or 'eche' or 'ilk'. Some of the best prose of the period was written in the West Midlands. Structurally, it forms an unbroken link between Anglo-Saxon prose and the prose of the early modern period. But its phonology had little influence on early Modern English, which derived its vowels and consonants mainly from the south-eastern speech of the London-Essex area. Over the whole apparently diversified area of Middle English speech and writing, there remains, in fact, a continuity of sentence pattern and stress and of English juncture. The best way to isolate these is to eliminate the dialectal variations in individual words and modernise the spelling.

The rhythmically stressed and heavily alliterated homiletic prose of persuasion continued its popularity for some time. The most striking set of texts in this style, the so-called 'Katherine Group', belong to the early thirteenth century. These, in a western speech, consist of the lives of three women martyrs, St. Katherine, St. Margaret, and St. Juliana. The EETS editor of the life of St. Margaret suggests that all three were written for delivery in a convent church. This suggestion finds confirmation in their contents and their prose style. These dramatic stories of the tribulations and resistance of martyred women were clearly adapted to an audience of nuns, and the obvious continuation of the Aelfric-Wulfstan style indicates an author familiar with the Anglo-Saxon elevated style of homiletic prose, as the following passages indicate:

þís me were léouere   ȝef þu wél wóldest
to hábben and to hálden þe   cwíc þen to acwéllen þe

This to me were better   if you would it well
To have and to hold you   living, than to kill you.   [*St. Catherine*][2]

And *b*id this *b*oon   Lord God almighty
My *m*irth and my *m*eed.   [*St. Juliana, mod. sp.*]³

The *w*ormes and the *w*ild deer
That in this *w*ood *w*onneth [dwell]
*L*ive after the *l*aw
That you them have *l*ooked [ordained]

This *m*aiden that we *m*unneth [commemorate]
Was *M*argaret ihaten [called]
And her *f*leshly *f*ather
Theodosie *h*ight
Of that *h*eathen folk
Patriarch and *p*rince
And she as the *d*earworth *D*ryhten [Lord] it *d*ight
Was *b*rought to a *b*orough
To *f*eed and to *f*oster
From that *m*ighty Antioch fifteen *m*iles.
                    [*St. Margaret, mod. sp.*]⁴

Closely allied in date and in style, though not so regularly alliterated is a treatise on virginity and the miseries of marriage, *Holy Maidenhood*, and an ecstatic address to Jesus (written for a 'leue suster'), *The Wooing of our Lord*:

Ah Jesu sweet Jesu
*L*eave that the *l*ove of thee
Be all my *l*iking
But *l*argess is *l*ittle worth
There *w*isdom *w*ants
                    [*Wooing of our Lord, mod. sp.*]⁵

Though this 'elevated' alliterative prose declined in popularity, it never completely disappeared. The pairing of words and alliteration remained a style of native pulpit eloquence that influenced the Book of Common Prayer in the sixteenth century and successive translations of the Bible. Echoes of it are still possible in Jeremy Taylor and other preachers of the seventeenth century.

Much more common in the early Middle English sermon was the continuation of Alfredian prose. The consciously rhetorical style of the Katherine group is exceptional. The majority of extant sermons from this part of the period, whether they are the old-fashioned anecdotal sermon

or the friars' 'syllogistic' sermon, assume a conversational tone and a
normal, virtually modern, sentence-structure. Twelfth-century examples
are found in the Trinity and Lambeth homilies, written in a style little
removed from the Alfredian prose of exposition:

> Thus maked our saviour his holy procession, from Betsage to Jeru-
> salem, and each Christian man maketh this day procession fro church
> to church and eft again, and betokeneth the holy procession that he
> maked this day.
>
> [*Trinity Homilies, mod. sp.*][6]

> Dear men, if you listen will and you willingly understand it, we you
> will sweetly say of the freedom that belongs to the day that is iclept
> Sunday. Sunday is ihaten [called] this Lord's Day and eek the day of
> bliss and lisse [ease] and of rest for all.
>
> [*Lambeth Homilies, mod. sp.*][7]

This remains basically the standard style of preaching throughout the
period. One further illustration a century later will suffice. It is from the
sermon of Dan Gaytryge, who like other priests of the time, had been
instructed by his bishop to preach 'openly, in English, upon Sundays':

> And he [i.e. the bishop] bids and commands in all that he may, that
> all that have cure or keeping under him move their parishioners and
> their subjects, that they hear and learn these same six things, and oft-
> times rehearse them till that they know them, and then teach them
> their children, if they any have, what time so they are of age to learn
> them.
>
> [*mod. sp.*][8]

As one moves from the thirteenth century to the later Middle English
period, one is conscious of a new influence on the plain prose of the
sermon. The Alfredian conversational sentence is still the basis. But it has
lengthened and the clean line has gone. The preacher draws breath (with
a phrase like 'the which' or 'wherein' or 'wherefor' or 'inasmuchas')
several times in the course of one sentence, and starts up again:

> But through protection of God's grace, he passed out of that pain as
> man unhurt, *wherefore* the same tyrant made him to be exiled into
> Patmos, *where* in a certain Sunday was shewed unto him by divine
> revelations the state of Holy Church and certain persecutions, *the
> which* should afterward befall in the world and of the damnation of
> the evil and glorification unto the good.
>
> [*mod. sp.*][9]

This is from an early fifteenth-century collection of model sermons written for priests who had no Latin, the *Speculum Sacerdotale*. This new trailing sentence-structure (which may run to several hundred words before the modern editor can find a place for a legitimate full-stop) is perhaps the natural consequence of a conversational style of writing developed by authors who had neither training in rhetoric nor an instinctive feeling for Alfredian prose. But the more immediate source was French. Some of the important Middle English prose homilies and manuals of instruction were translated from French originals, which have left an impact on their syntax.

The influence can be seen as early as the thirteenth century in a set of Kentish sermons, which were translated from the French of Maurice de Sully, who had been Bishop of Paris. The passage from Matthew 8 already cited in Chapter Three will serve for illustration. The West-Saxon Gospels had written:

Drihten, hæle us; we mote forwurþan.

Both the Wycliffe and the Tyndale versions preserve the characteristic English juncture between 'us' and 'we', and it is repeated in the Authorised Version:

Lord, save us: we perish.

The Bishop of Paris, however, had an explanatory link-word at this point – 'kar' – the modern French *car*:

Sire sauue nos *kar* nos perisons.

In the Kentish version this French locution is picked up:

Lord save us, *for* we perisheth.

[*mod. sp.*

On occasion the version is so close to French as to be in dubious English idiom:

And *so* they were in the ship, *so* arose a great tempest

[*mod. sp.*]

which blindly echoes the French:

Et *si* cum il furent en la mier, *si* leua un grant torment.[10]

One of the most influential French treatises in the period was the *Somme des Vices et des Vertus* (or the *Somme le Roi*) by a thirteenth-century Dominican friar. After Peckhams's Constitutions of Lambeth of 1281, numerous English versions were made as a kind of text-book for the instruction of laymen by parish priests. (Dan Michel's *Ayenbit of Inwit* of 1340 and Caxton's *Royal Book* of 1486 are both versions of it). The EETS version

The Book of Vices and Virtues, which prints parallel pages of French and English, illustrates with great clarity this new fashion of using the link-words of the trailing mediaeval French syntax in place of the natural English openings of clauses.[11] *Cest a dire* produces 'that is to say'; *Car* produces 'for'; *au regart de* produces 'as to'; *dont* (mod. French *donc* produces 'and therefore'; the variations of *lequel* produce the 'the which', 'to the which', 'for the which' that lie so thickly on the pages of much late Middle English prose. The trailing sentence (and again the influence is a French original) lasts at least as long as Caxton at the end of the fifteenth century.

Standing apart from the sermon, whether alliterative or conversational, is the great monument of early Middle English prose, the *Ancrene Riwle*, on which R. W. Chambers has written with some eloquence. There is no trace of French syntax or of Anglo-Saxon alliterative prose. It is a direct development (written in the West of England where the tradition was strongest) of Alfredian prose. Written originally in the late twelfth century for three young women who had retreated from the world, it was revised (as the *Ancrene Wisse*) about 1230 for a larger community of nuns. Its importance was such that it reversed the usual practice of the time and was translated into both Latin and French. It is a compendium of homiletic instruction for life within the walls, but the author has a lively interest (which he nevertheless persuades his three maidens against) in the actual world. His imagery illuminates aspect after aspect of mediaeval life – the siege of a castle with boiling water thrown from the towers, the goldsmith at work, the house on fire from a casual spark, the animals on the farm and the fleas on the dog, the market, the granary, the stinking privy. He can teach with homely details, etch a mordant character study, or sound a note of Donne-like warning with equal effectiveness:

> Wherefore the anchoress, what so she be, as much as she ever can and may, let her hold her stillness; let her have not the nature of the hen. The hen, when it has laid, knows but to cackle. And what profits her thereof? Comes the chough anon and rieveth her her eggs, and eats all that of what she should have brought forth her living birds; and right as the wicked chough, the devil bears away from the cackling anchoresses and swallows all the good that they have brought forth, that should as birds bear them up toward heaven, if it had not been cackled. The wretched pedlar more noise he maketh to cry his soap than a rich mercer all his dearworth ware.

> [*mod. sp.*]

The greedy glutton is the fiend's manciple. For he sticketh ever in the cellar or in the kitchen. His heart is in the dishes; his thought is all on the cloth; his life in the tun; his soul in the crock. Cometh forth before his Lord besmutted and besmeared, a dish in his one hand, a bowl in his other. Babbleth with words, and wiggleth as a drunken man that mindeth to fall, beholds his great belly; and the fiend laugheth that he bursteth.

[*mod. sp.*]

The proud be his [the devil's] trumpeters, draw wind inward of worldly praise, and then, with idle boasting, puff it outwards, as the trumpeter doth, to make noise, loud blazon to shew their pride. But if they well thought of God's trumpeters and of the angels' trumpets of heaven, that shall in four quarters of the world before the dread doom grisly blow, 'Arise, dead, arise! Come to God's doom to be judged, where no proud trumpeter can be redeemed' – if they thought this well, they would soon enough in the devil's service more dimly blow.

[*mod. sp.*][12]

In passages such as these (and they are typical of the whole work) we are face to face with an author who is in the central tradition of English prose. He is not, in the modern sense, a literary author. But he can write; and the prose which he so nobly served stood ready for the moment – and it was not far off – when prose was to invade the literary territories that had been hitherto reserved for verse.

With the fourteenth century we are into a time when English prose is the accepted medium, not only for the world of religion, but also for public affairs. It was tolerated in the law courts and encouraged in the schools. English wills appear. The regulations of the various guilds begin to be written in the native tongue. In this setting, one can anticipate that English will become a medium for secular writing, and so one finds it in the prose of the Trevisa, 'Mandeville', and Chaucer.

Yet none of these are major writers of prose. Trevisa writes with a competent bluntness:

All the language of the Northumbrians, and especially at York, is so sharp, slitting and frotting, and unshaped, that we Southern men can that language scarcely understand.

[*mod. sp.*][13]

But useful though his information is, there is a mechanical plodding dullness in his writing. 'Mandeville' is never dull. Translating from a French original he writes (in the guise of a travel book) prose fiction of the most unlikely marvels. The contents of Mandeville still fascinate, but his prose is (even in modern spelling) 'quaint'. It has what appears to be an archaic flavour compared with the modernity of the *Ancrene Riwle*. The reason is not archaism, but his leaning on his French original. His sentences have no firm line. They begin with 'and' or 'now therefor' or 'that is' or 'forasmuch as' or 'for' (a favourite opening – from French *car* again):

> *And* man shall bear the diamond on his left side. *For* it is of greater virtue then, than on the right side. *For* the strength of their growing is toward the North, *that is* the left side of the world, and the left party of man, is when he turneth his face toward the East.
>
> [*mod. sp.*][14]

The prose of Chaucer has no touch of the genius he showed in his other works. It is Chaucer, rather than Milton, of the English poets who wrote prose with his left hand. One can discount his *Boethius*, which is a translation, and his *Parson's Tale*, which is pastiche-sermon in the current trailing style. But his *Treatise on the Astrolabe* (when one compares it with the crisp expositional prose of the Anglo-Saxon *Leechdoms*) has the stop-and-start movement of so much of the Frenchified prose of his time:

> The plate under the riet [net] is discrived with 3 principal cercles, o, *which* the leest is clepid the cercle of Cancre *by cause that* the heved [head] of Cancre turnith evermo consentrik upon the same cercle. In this heved of Cancre is the grettist declinacioun northward of the sonne, *and therfore* is he clepid solsticium of somer; *which* declinacioun, after Ptholome, is 23 degrees and 50 minutes as wel in Cancer as in Capricorn ...
> Take there thin altitude meridian, *that is to seyn*, the highest of the sonne as for that day.[15]

Chaucer is, admittedly, dealing with quite a complex problem of exposition. But one has a certain sympathy for 'little Lewis my son' for whom this snake-like prose was written.

In spite of the fourteenth-century spread of prose into secular writing, the clerics remain the better writers. The three contemplative mystics, Rolle, Hilton, and (though to a lesser extent) the unknown author of *The Cloud of Unknowing*, continue what the *Ancrene Riwle* had established, an idiomatic native prose equally adapted for reading or for private listening. Rolle's prose is essentially modern in sentence-structure:

Wherefor, accordingly, Aristotle says that some fowls are of good flying, that pass from one land to another; some are of ill flying, for heaviness of body, and because their nest is not far from the earth. Thus it is of them that turn them to God's service. Some are of good flying, for they fly from earth to heaven, and rest them there in thought, and are fed in delight of God's love, and have thought of no love of the world. Some are that can not fly from this land, but on the way let their heart rest, and delight them in many loves of men and women.

[ROLLE, *mod. sp.*][16]

Hilton can add a touch of rhetoric to the basic prose style:

Lo, I set you in the right way: this is the way, and that you keep the learning that I ken you. What so you hear or feel or see that should let you on the way, bide not with it wilfully, tarry not for it restfully, behold it not, like it not, dread it not; but aye go forth on the way and think that you would be at Jerusalem.

[HILTON, *mod. sp.*][17]

The Cloud of Unknowing, which has been the subject of somewhat exaggerated estimates, does not compare with Rolle or Hilton. The tone is conversational, and the vocabulary everyday, but the sentences tend to trail:

A young disciple in God's school, new turned from the world, *the which* weeneth that for a little time he has given himself to penance and to prayer, taken by counsel in confession, that he be therefore able to take upon him ghostly working, *of the which* he heareth men speak or read about him *or peradventure* readeth himself ...

[*mod. sp.*][18]

The whole sentence continues in this manner for a total of some four hundred words. Indeed, though the author usually writes well, he sometimes anticipates the disorganised rambling style of some of the writers of the fifteenth century. But in general his prose is more effective than that of his secular contemporaries, and with his fellow mystics he is in the central tradition of English prose-writing.

Wycliffe and his followers form a special group. Their unorthodox Lollard views were suppressed by the Church, and many of Wycliffe's works were burnt early in the fifteenth century. Yet the 'Wycliffite' translation of the Bible into English survives in many manuscripts. Wycliffe, like many parish priests, saw English as the language of instruction, but he went further than they could venture, insisting that laymen should have access to the Bible in their own tongue. Inevitably, this involved not only translation, but controversy, and his original English works are mainly tracts, written in a prose that echoes the natural speech of his lay audience. If the *Ancrene Riwle* represents one side of continuity, the persistence of the homiletic tradition, the conversational mode of Wycliffe's tracts represents the other, the continuity of the spoken tongue. Even the manuscript spelling (here largely preserved) cannot conceal the closeness of fourteenth-century spoken prose to the sentence-structure of the present day:

> The Holy Gost gaf to apostlis wit at Whit-Sunday for to knowe al maner langagis to teche the puple Goddis lawe therby: and so God wolde that the puple were taught Goddis lawe in dyverse tungis; but what man on Goddis half shulde reverse Goddis ordenaunse and his wille? And for this cause seynt Jerome travelide and translatide the Bible fro dyverse tungis into Latin that it myghte be aftir translatid to othere tungis. And thus Christ and his apostlis taughten the puple in that tunge that was moost knowun to the puple; why shulden not men do nou so?[19]

Three and a half centuries after the Conquest, good written English prose, based on the conversational norm, has survived everything from official apathy to overt discouragement. The men and women who had no position or power, and who merely spoke the language, proved in the end to be the most influential patrons. Three distinctive prose styles had emerged in the period: the alliterative rhetorical style, which gradually fell into disuse except as an occasional mannerism; the continuation, in the homilies and the Wycliffe group, of Alfredian prose, with its 'normal' word-order and a relatively short sentence made up of one or two main clauses with subordinate clauses integrally related; and finally a new kind of prose (both religious and secular) influenced by French originals, where the sentence tends to become a considerable accumulation of main and subordinate statements linked by connectives like 'for' or 'that is to say' or 'inasmuch as' translated directly from French.

The Alfredian sentence, and its Middle English continuation, has a coherent unity. It achieves communication with syntactical compactness. The adjective clause is firmly joined to its antecedent, the noun clause stands close to its verb, the time or reason adverbial clause comes early. The writer gives the impression of having thought out the whole statement before he put pen to paper. In the new trailing sentence the unity and coherence have gone. The syntax is disjointed. The reason for an action follows the action in a kind of explanatory afterthought. Each clause seems to generate the next one, which gives no impression of its having been in the writer's mind when he began the sentence. The Alfredian sentence looks forward purposefully to its conclusion. The writer of the trailing sentence is continually looking backwards over his shoulder at what has gone before and then adding something further, a reason, an explanation, a consequence, or even a further statement.

When the next century opens, both styles are available, and English prose is poised for the next move. But it was to be no simple series of forward steps. There was no forecasting which sentence-structure would predominate. English writers in the fifteenth century are committed to English, both by national feeling and by new literary ambitions, but they are still hunting, even groping, for a generally agreed and acceptable way of writing prose. The continuous central tradition (Alfredian prose to Middle English homiletic writing and 'spoken' prose and so to early modern) is clear to anyone looking back from the standpoint of the late seventeenth century. But it was not clear to English writers at the close of the Middle Ages, and the fifteenth century is in prose an age of restless experimentation, which deserves a brief chapter to itself.

Notes

1   G. R. OWST, *Preaching in Mediaeval England*, Cambridge, 1926, Ch. 6.
2   *Life of St. Katherine*, ed. E. EINENKEL, EETS, 1884, 92.
3   J. HALL, ed., *Early Middle English*, Oxford, 1920, i, 147, 'Saint Juliana'.
4   *Seinte Marharete*, ed. F. M. MACK, EETS, 1934, 5.
5   *Þe Wohunge of Ure Lauerd*, in OE Homilies ed. R. MORRIS, EETS, 1868, 271.
6   *Old English Homilies* (Trinity MS), ed. R. MORRIS, EETS, 1873, 91.
7   *Old English Homilies* (Lambeth MS), ed. R. MORRIS, EETS, 1868, 41.
8   *Religious Pieces* (including Dan John Gaytryge's Sermon), EETS, 1867, 2.
9   *Speculum Sacerdotale*, ed. E. H. WEATHERLY, EETS, 1936, 11.
10 J. HALL, ed., *Early Middle English*, Oxford, 1920, i, 219: ii, 669.
11 *The Book of Vices and Virtues*, ed. W. N. FRANCIS, EETS, 1942, xliff.
12 *The English Text of the Ancrene Riwle*, ed. M. DAY, EETS, 1952, 28–9, 95–6, 93–4.
13 K. SISAM, ed., *Fourteenth Century Verse and Prose*, Oxford, 1921, 150; Trevisa, translation of Higden.
14 SISAM, *op. cit.*, 98. Mandeville.
15 F. N. ROBINSON, ed., *The Works of Chaucer*, London, 1933, 644, 650.
16 SISAM, *op. cit.*, 42. Rolle.
17 *Hilton's The Scale of Perfection*, ed. E. UNDERHILL, London, 1921, ii, 21.
18 *The Cloud of Unknowing*, ed. P. HODGSON, EETS, 1944, 95.
19 *Wycliffe, English Works (De Officio Pastorali)*, ed. F. D. MATTHEWS, EETS, 1880, 429.

Chapter 6
The Fifteenth Century

The essential feature of fifteenth-century prose is the emergence of English as the main written medium. In 1422 the London brewers decided to abandon Latin in their records and use 'our mother-tongue, to wit the English tongue', citing with approbation the example of Henry V, who 'hath with a diligent mind procured the common idiom (setting aside others) to be commended by the exercise of writing'.[1] This decision by a guild of London citizens had far-reaching implications. The brewers represented a social class whose rising importance in the century set the seal on the acceptance of the English language. They had always spoken English. Now they will write it – and read it. For this new literate group there was no lack of schooling. Alongside the fifteenth-century grammar schools, which taught Latin to the future cleric, there had grown up a series of vernacular schools, 'petty schools', and small schools organised by chantry and parish priests. The lesser country gentlemen, the merchants, and (what is perhaps more important) their wives and their servants, could by the opening of the century set pen to paper, keep records and accounts, and write letters with complete assurance. This general ability to write English extends to more public documents. Wills are now commonly written in English;[2] and English, of a colloquial and direct quality, is used in the ordinances of the various guilds.[3] Written English prose is no longer regarded merely as a concession for un-Latined religious women. It became, in the fifteenth century, a necessity for everyday living.

The main movement of English prose in this century is seen not so much in formal set works as in the day-to-day documents. The speech which had been orally preserved is now transferred, often verbatim, to paper. At the end of the century, Caxton and his immediate successors printed some thousands of separate volumes of English prose. From Caxton's day to the present, the printed book has made these titles relatively easy of access, and it is tempting to assume that in Caxton's pages we can find the main currents of the time embodied in an authoritative corpus of our earlier prose. Nothing could be further from the truth. The early printers published prose only within a limited range. Caxton, indeed, concentrated largely on translation, and much of what he put out bears in consequence the continual imprint of another language. If we are to examine what was really being written in English prose in the fifteenth century, what lay behind the great writing of the next two centuries, we must go beyond what the first printers thought worth setting up on their presses.

It is possible to distinguish three major varieties of prose written in the period. Firstly, there is the prose that is based directly on, or never very far removed from, the natural speech of the day. It can range in content from mere trivia to work of importance. Secondly, there is a considerable body of what is essentially 'written' prose, produced by industrious translators working from Latin or French originals. From this mass of manuscripts a few translations like Nicholas Love's *Mirrour of the Blessed Lyf of Jesu Christ* stand out for the quality of their writing. The great majority of them are little more than painstaking and sometimes mechanical cribs. Finally, there are the conscious stylists, of whom Caxton, Pecock, Fortesque, and Malory are the best examples. To call them conscious stylists does not mean that they all write what we can now regard as good English prose – Caxton is a generally clumsy writer and Pecock is an oddity. But they were all conscious that there was a problem, and their varying solutions of the style appropriate for written English form the pattern of experimentation that characterises the latter part of the century. The feel of the Renaissance is already in the air.

Prose is written in response to a need. The earlier need for homilies and saints' lives continued. But the general tone of fifteenth-century prose is secular. Even much of the religious writing is directed to the layman rather than to the professional cleric. His needs were further filled by such ventures as the re-establishment of the prose chronicle (which recovered for him his English history), the books on proper behaviour (which made easier his upward movement in the social scale), and the innumerable manuals on all aspects of the technology of the time, from home medicine to hunting and cutting open a stag. There was no literary pretension about this kind of writing. Prose was there to be useful. It was perhaps because of this that much of the prose of the period has the kind of professional anonymity today associated with journalism.

Prose of the Spoken Norm

Here is a recipe for apple fritters:

Fritours: Take yolkes of egges, drawe hem thorgh a streynour, caste thereto faire floure, berme and ale; stere it togidre til hit be thik. Take pared appelles, cut hem thyn like obleies [wafers], lay hem in the batur; then put hem into a ffrying-pan and fry hem in faire grece or buttur till thei ben browne yelowe; then put hem in disshes, and strawe sugur on hem ynogh, And serve hem forthe.[4]

The date is fifteenth century. The sentence-structure and most of the vocabulary could be found in the Leechdoms in the tenth century; they could equally be found in Mrs Beeton in the nineteenth. This relatively unchanged and unchanging style does little more than echo the imperatives of English speech of any period. Whether imperative or narrative, it was being written regularly by master and servant, husband and wife throughout the century, as the great volumes of the Cely, Paston and Stonor letters show. The Pastons in particular move with an easy freedom from the formal phrases of the conventional letter of the period ('Right worshipful husband, I commend me to you' ... 'The Trinity have you in his keeping, and send you good speed in all your matters') to the needs of the moment in the most conversational of structures:

Husband to wife:
There is a white box with evidence of Stratton in one of the canvas bags in the great coffer, or in the spruce chest. Ric. Calle knows it well, and there is a deed of feoffment and a letter of attorney made of the same lands ...

Son to father:
I send you home Pecock again. He is not for me ... you shall have knowledge afterward how he hath demened him here with me. I would, saving your displeasure, that you were delivered of him, for he shall never do you profit or worship.

Wife to husband:
I pray you to get some cross-bows and windacs to bind them with and quarrels [bolts]; for your houses here been so low that there may no man shoot out with no long bow, though we had never so much need ... I pray you that you will vouchsafe to do buy for me 1lb. of almonds and 1lb. of sugar, and that you will do buy some freize to make of your child his gowns. You shall have best cheap and best choice of Hay's wife, as is told me. And that you will buy a yard of broad cloth of black for a hood for me of 44d or 4s a yard, for there is neither good cloth nor good freize in this town.

[*mod. sp.*][5]

From the letters of the period it is only a step to the 'writings' of Margery Kempe produced in the 1430's. Of formal education she appears to have had none. She had to dictate to a couple of clerks her astonishing narrative of marital dissension, pilgrimages to overseas shrines, and mystic experience. She has remarkable narrative skill and an instinctive judgement of effective oral prose:

> The seyd creatur, lying in her bed the next nyth folwing, herd with her bodily erys a lowde voys clepyng 'Margery'. With that voys sche woke, gretly aferyd, and, lying stille in sylens, sche mad hir preyerys as deuowtly as sche cowde for the tyme.[6]

The opening of the second sentence, with its deft reference backwards in a parenthetic phrase (with *that* voice ...) demonstrates the taut native construction. Caxton would have written 'with *the which* voice', and lost the narrative tension.

Oral prose produced in the period what can almost be described as a fifteenth-century genre, the short story. It had its beginnings in the mediaeval exemplum, the story inserted in the sermon to point a moral and engage the listeners' attention. At the beginning of the century Mirk produced his *Festial*. In form it is the typical collection of homilies for various saints' days that had been common in the fourteenth century. Mirk, however, spends little time on exposition of doctrine. For him the 'narracio', or inset story, is the important part, and the *Festial* is largely a tissue of lively colloquial narratives, as in this tale of a puzzled 'maystyr of diuinyte':

> Then, on a day, as he walked by the seaside deeply studying in this matter, he was ware of a fair child sitting on the sea-sand, and had made a little pit in the sand, and with his hand with a little shell he took of the sea water and poured into that pit. Then thought this master he was a fool for to do so, and spoke to him, and said, 'Son, whereabouts art thou?' Then said he, 'Sir, I am about for to held [pour] all the water in the sea into this pit'. Then said the master, 'Leave off, son, for thou shalt never do that.' 'Sir', quoth he again, 'I shall as soon do this, as thou shalt do that that you are about'.
>
> [*mod. sp.*][7]

From Mirk to the collection of stories detached from the sermon framework was a short transition, and there are many examples of such collections in the century. Two of the most notable are *An Alphabet of Tales* and the very popular *Gesta Romanorum*. Ostensibly they are still for the use of preachers – each tale in the *Gesta* concludes with a 'moralitas'. But their great popularity arose from their value as racily told colloquial stories. Most of them come from Latin originals. Unlike the longer saints' lives of the time (where the Latin still shows through the English translation) the language and sentence-structure of the short story are completely native. Here is the ending of the story of a small boy, brought up in ignorance of the world, and particularly of women. When he is brought face to face with women, he is told they are 'devils that deceive men':

> And when he had seen all manner of things, they brought him unto the king his father; and he asked him of all things that he had seen, which he loved best. And he answered again and said, 'Father, forsooth, nothing else but devils that deceive men, for of them alonely before all other is my heart set.'
>
> [*mod. sp.*][8]

This native genre of the short-story collection finally lost all contact with the sermon and from *A Hundred Mery Tales* in the early sixteenth century, to Tarleton, Joe Miller, and beyond, it became part of the oral folk-lore of England. It will, in time, become part of the fabric of the novel.

In the fifteenth century the chronicle written in English was revived. The Old English chronicle had lapsed in the twelfth century. In the intervening years Latin was the medium of the historians. The new assured status of English made an English chronicle inevitable, and a beginning is seen in *The Brut*. Although the earlier part of *The Brut* was derived from the French *Brut d'Engleterre*, both the translated sections and the later additions (to 1479) fall instinctively into the rhythms and structures of Alfredian prose:

> He was led to the Tower of London, and laid upon a hurdle and drawn through the City to Tyburn gallows, and there hanged, and let down again all quick, and his bowels cut out of his body, and burned before him. And then was his head smitten off, and his body quartered; and one sent to Oxford, the second sent to Cambridge, the third to Bristol, and the fourth to [blank in MS]; and his head was set upon London Bridge, and thus he ended his life in this world.
>
> [1442 entry, *mod. sp.*][9]

John Capgrave's *The Chronicle of England*, of somewhat later date, continues the record of the savagery of the times in what had now become established as the chronicle style:

> Then were take and slain thousands. The King was in the field soon

after midnight. This espied Cobham; he fled; and many with him. Many of his were take, and hang, and draw, and brent.

[1414 entry, *mod. sp.*][10]

The chronicle is to become virtually an art form in such later writers as Fabyan, Hall, and Holinshed. The style once established, however, remained the traditional manner of writing for this kind of direct historical narrative.

The demand in the fifteenth century for manuals of instruction was insatiable. There is hardly an aspect of the life of the times on which a manuscript treatise does not survive. Surgery, medicine, the herbal, hunting, hawking, cooking, instructions for travelling pilgrims, manuals of behaviour, these are only a few of the 'text-books' provided, not for the professional (who could read his Latin) but for the enquiring layman. Inevitably the language and the style are simple and direct.

A few examples must suffice to illustrate this fifteenth-century prose of exposition and instruction. *The Master of Game* in the early years of the century and *The Book of St. Albans* in its later years were treatises on the interests of gentlemen – hawking, hunting, the blazoning of arms, and 'fishing with an angle'. The readers were more likely to be country squires than town merchants. But the country gentry found in these volumes the direct English exposition already demanded by the London brewers, and this in spite of the French original of the earlier book. In both, the language is clear, precise and workmanlike, and the sentence-structure conversational and uncomplicated:

And then should the hunter flay down the skin as far as he can, and then with a sharp trencher cut as thick as he can the flesh down to the neck-bone, and this done every man stand abroad and blow the death, and make short bay for to reward the hounds.

[*Master of Game, mod. sp.*][11]

In both books the many instructions for the cure of sick animals echo the Leechdoms faithfully:

Take the powdre of Saxifrage; or ellys the powdre of rewe, and a quantyte of May butter and tempre it well togider till they ben evyn medled. Then put it in a lyttle boxe and stoppe it faste. And as ofte as ye fede your hawke an hoole meele, anoynt her meete a lytyll therwyth and that shall make her love meete the better, for love of the oynement.

[*Book of St. Albans*][12]

The 1496 printed edition of *The Book of St. Albans* contained an extra section on 'fishing with an angle', the prose of which is undisguisedly Alfredian:

> The carpe is a deyntous fysshe; but there ben but fewe in Englonde. And therefore I write the lasse of hym. He is an evyll fysshe to take.[13]

For one fifteenth-century writer, this simple, expository, 'spoken' prose was a deliberate choice. Sir John Fortescue, after a lifetime of legal practice and of writing in Latin on constitutional problems, set down in English (in the 1470's) his final views on political philosophy, *The Governance of England*. He avoided all Latin and French sentence-structures, and where he had to use French legal terms he was careful to insert an English explanation. Fortescue, apart from his importance as our earliest writer on political science, emerges as one of the main writers of prose in the century. His solution for effective expository prose is a series of short sentences in Alfredian sentence-structure, with a minimum of foreign borrowing of vocabulary:

> Ther is no man hanged in Scotlande in vij yere to gedur ffor robbery. And yet thai ben often tymes hanged for larceny, and stelynge off good in the absence of the owner theroff. But ther hartes serve hem not to take a manys gode, while he is present, and woll defende it; wich maner of takynge is callid robbery. But the Englysh man is of another corage.[14]

This is not the unaffected transcribed gossip of the Pastons. It is a controlled, literary, style; but it is based on the movement of the same kind of speech, albeit the deliberate speech of a man thinking slowly and carefully. Fortescue's skill in advancing his argument and in explaining his technical terms as he goes along without clumsiness and without breaking the line of his sentences, is very impressive. *The Governance of England* is a real landmark in the history of English prose.

'Written Prose'

Alongside this prose based on the spoken norm, there was produced in the fifteenth century a vast amount of prose based on Latin or French written originals. The fifteenth century rivalled the later Tudor period in the sheer bulk of translation into English. But while the Tudor translator was engaged in translating literary classics into English of lively and idiomatic elegance, the fifteenth-century translator was strictly utilitarian in his attitudes. He had seldom any interest in English style. So long as he rendered the content of the saint's life or homily or manual into English words he was content. On the whole, those who worked from Latin originals produced better English prose. The sentence-structure of the Latin was so far removed from English that they were forced to rethink the sentence and give it some kind of English shape. Capgrave in his *Life of St. Gilbert*, *The Revelations of St. Birgitta* and Nicholas Love in *The Mirrour of the Blessed Lyf of Jesu* rise above the general level of translation in the period. Their English *is* English:

> He bade his disciples take the ship and go into the water before him; and then he alone went up in to the hill.
>
> [*The Mirrour ... of Jesu, mod. sp.*][15]

> Lynen cloth hath ij goodes: first, it is softe and esy to the bare bodye; secunde, it leseth nott hys coloure, bot the ofter it is wesh, the clenner it is.
>
> [*St. Birgitta*][16]

Nicholas Love, though writing in the first few years of the century, catches often the movement of the Latin periodic sentence, long before the English Renaissance made such a movement commonplace:

> And so we may see if we take good heed by devout compassion in what mischief and tribulation they were at that time, both for the great tempest that was risen upon them, and also for the night's time, and principally for they lacked the lordes presence that was all their refute in their need.[17]   [*mod. sp.*]

The translators from French are almost universally characterised by their helpless dependence on the phrasing and sentence-structure of the originals. The syntax of French by now was close enough to that of English for the one language to be translated, word by word and unit by unit into the other, to produce a kind of machine-translation that was at least understandable. The end-result bore no relationship to idiomatic spoken English. An excellent example can be seen in *The Dictes and Sayings of the Philosophers*, which Caxton printed in 1477. This was a collection of the sayings of ancient writers, translated twice from French in the century. The earlier translation in 1450 by Stephen Scrope bears all the traces of the item-by-item machine-translation of the period. Caxton's version was done by Earl Rivers. Though only twenty years separate the two versions, Rivers looks forward to the elegance and native idiom of the Tudors; Scrope's English is absolutely controlled by the French:

Ypocras fut disciple de Esculapius le secont,
Ipocras was Esculapius disciple   the secound,

et fut de la lignie le premier, de la quelle lignie
and was the first of the lyne,   of the which lyne

furent deux roys
were   ij   kingis.[18]

Rivers, faced with the same French, compresses the whole material into an assured two-clause English sentence:

Ypocras was disciple to Esculapius the second which descended of blode royall.[19]

Scrope rather than Rivers is the typical fifteenth-century translator, and this 'written' English is everywhere evident, in the translated homilies and saints' lives, in manuals and courtesy-books like the *Book of the Knight of La Tour-Landry*.

When the first printing press was established in Westminster, it was to this 'written' material and not to the spoken that Caxton turned. He himself was a considerable translator. He writes with feeling of his handicaps, his birth in Kent where English was 'brode and rude', his thirty years' residence in the Low Countries, the sheer bulk of the material which made him 'halfe desperate' to complete the great mediaeval collection of saints' lives, *The Golden Legend*.[20] Caxton is an honest and conscientious technician. He does not write well. He recognises that there were problems, the unstable English of his time, and the technical difficulties of translation. Yet to the end of his career he is an exponent of the 'written' style. His French originals shape his every phrase. Even in his prologues and epilogues, which generally have no original, the trailing sentence studded with 'which', 'wherefore', 'the which', 'that is to say', 'and also' as the links between the clauses is the staple. As he grew older, he sometimes attained a more colloquial grip on his language, as in the prologue to *Eneydos* of 1490 with its illuminating discussion of the linguistic problems of his day. Caxton's great contribution to English is that of the grand entrepreneur. From his prose, and the whole 'written' medium which it represents, there was to be no issue.

The Conscious Stylists

However hard he might work at his written prose, Caxton's thirty years away from England had ruined his ear for the movement of English speech. At the other end of the scale, Fortescue had achieved for exposition a deliberate colloquial prose of great power. Two other writers of the century, Malory and Pecock, faced with equal consciousness the problem of creating an appropriate written style. Malory's solution was to turn to the past, both for his Arthurian material and for his vocabulary and syntax. He uses a sequence of words that are often monosyllabic for whole sentences at a time. His vocabulary is predominantly Anglo-Saxon. Latin borrowings are rare and French words infrequent. His sentence-structure is paratactic or co-ordinate, with 'and' as the favourite link. The whole style is a deliberate artefact. It does not represent the language of his own day. Equally it is not the language of any earlier period. And yet it is extraordinarily successful. The narrative of *Morte D'Arthur* moves with langour or speed as the action requires; the meditative moments are profound; the great climaxes and speeches are intensely moving:

> 'A, Launcelot!' he sayd, 'thou were hede of al Crysten knyghtes! And now I dare say', sayd syr Ector, 'thou sir Launcelot, there thou lyest, that thou were never matched of erthely knyghtes hande. And thou were the curtest knyght that ever bare shelde! And thou were the truest frende to thy lovar that ever bestrade hors, and thou were the trewest lover of a synful man that ever loved woman, and thou were the kyndest man that ever strake wyth swerde. And thou were the godelyest persone that ever cam emonge prees of knyghtes, and thou was the mekest man and the jentyllest that ever ete in halle emonge ladyes, and thou were the sternest knyght to thy mortal foo that ever put spere in the reeste.'
> Then there was wepyng and dolour out of mesure.[21]

In the middle years of the century Reginald Pecock, Bishop successively of St. Asaph and of Chichester, turned from Latin to English to defend the Church against the Lollards (*Repressor of over much blaming of the clergy*) and to expound the intricacies of theology to laymen (*The Donet, The Folower to the Donet*). Not for him the simplicity of Fortescue. The preaching tradition had left him with a love of words, rhythmically grouped in pairs or threes – 'writeth and holdeth', 'containeth, comprehendeth or closeth', 'conceit and consideration'. His recognition of the complexities of his subject led him to introduce caveats, expansions of meanings, and discussions of side-issues all in the one vast sentence. His deliberate avoidance of a learned Latin vocabulary precipitated him into the other extreme of inventing technical terms based on Anglo-Saxon, words like 'unstondabilnes' (instability), 'agenseie' (contradict), 'untobethoughtupon' (inconceivable), even less familiar to his contemporary readers. Pecock faced manfully up to the problems of creating an appropriate English style. On occasion he can be effective:

> What was Aristotil oþir þan a louer of trouþ, and þerfore a laborer bisi forto fynde þe knowyng of treuþ, boþe for him silf and for oþire?[22]

This is exceptional. The typical Pecock sentence is a long one. It does not trail. Pecock's mind was too disciplined for that. It tacks and veers with the continual interpolations of a logical mind. The result is a dead prose, lacking in colour (which Pecock did not want) but lacking also in expositional force (which he did):

> Son, I cannot see but that, as into the purpose of thy question and into thine intent, all one it is whether they begin for to proffer to thee and thou their proffer accept, or thou begin for to proffer to them and they thy proffer accept; forwhy in ever-either case thou art constrained, for in ever-either case thou art put betwixt two evils or betwixt two things to be done, of which never-neither thou else wouldst do, and thou choosest it which seemeth to thee as then and so the less evil, for to avoid the greater evil ...[23]
>
> [*mod. sp.*]

The sentence thereafter marches steadfastly to its logical goal. It was not a sentence-structure that held any hope either then or for the future. Pecock is a gallant and lone worker whose experiments did not come off.

The fifteenth century is not usually thought of as an age of ferment. Yet in English prose the yeast was steadily working. The translators, even the poorest of them, brought the matter of Europe to the English reader. The best of them gained some sense of the major prose unit from the better Latin models. The experimenters and stylists, even when they had no later influence, were at least conscious that there was a series of technical problems involved, Fortescue and Malory solving theirs with great skill. Above all, the century put a pen in the hand of the layman and he instinctively transferred his speech to paper.

By the end of the century the last of the major influences on English prose was at work. Caxton writes in 1490, with admiration and perhaps even a little envy, of Skelton, who had recently translated Diodorus Siculus, 'not in rude and olde langage but in polysshed and ornate termes'. The contrast implied in this antithesis can be seen in the two earliest English versions of *The Imitation of Christ*. The early fifteenth-century version had translated 'gulosi ingenti siti ac fame cruciabuntur' into the 'rude and old language' of simple 'spoken' prose:

Gluttonous men shall be tormented with great hunger and great thirst.

The century had just closed when William Atkinson 'translated' the same Latin:

The glutton that hath consumed meats and drinks superflously to the detriment of their body and the injury of the poor that famished for hunger, then shall they famish for hunger in so much that if they wolde desire a drop of water to mitigate that exceeding ardour that they shall suffer, then it shall not be possible for them to attain it.

[*mod. sp.*]24

This is 'polished and ornate terms'. It is also something else. It is a new conception of the sentence. English prose is preparing to reach out and meet as an equal the new Latinity of the humanists.

Notes

1 R. W. CHAMBERS, & M. DAUNT, ed. *London English 1384–1425*, Oxford, 1931, 139.
2 *The Fifty Earliest English Wills*, ed. F. J. FURNIVALL, EETS, 1882.
3 *The Original Ordinances of the Early English Gilds*, ed. TOULMIN SMITH, EETS, reprint 1962.
4 *Two Fifteenth Century Cookery Books*, ed. T. AUSTEN, EETS, 1888, 73.
5 J. GAIRDNER, ed. *The Paston Letters*, London, 1904, iii, 298: iii, 302; ii, 101–2.
6 *The Booke of Margery Kempe*, ed. S. B. MEECH and H. E. ALLEN, EETS, 1940, 131.
7 *Mirk's Festial*, ed. T. ERBE, EETS, 1905, 167.
8 *An Alphabet of Tales*, ed. M. M. BANK, EETS, 1904–5, 119.
9 *The Brut*, ed. F. W. D. BRIE, EETS, 1906–8, 481.
10 F. C. HINGESTON, ed. *John Capgrave's The Chronicle of England*, London, 1888, 309.
11 W. & F. BAILIE-GROHMAN, *The Master of Game*, 1909, 174–5.
12 BERNERS, *The Book of Hawking, Hunting, and Blasing of Arms*, facs. by W. BLADES, London, 1905.
13 M. G. WATKINS, ed. *Treatyse of Fysshynge*, London, 1880.
14 C. PLUMMER, ed. *Fortescue's The Governance of England*, London, 1885, 142.
15 L. F. POWELL, ed., *N. Love's The Mirrour of the Blessed Lyf of Jesu Christ*, Oxford, 1908.
16 *The Revelations of St. Birgitta*, ed. W. P. CUMMINGS, EETS, 1929, 17.
17 POWELL, *op. cit.*
18 *Dictes and Sayings of the Philosophers*, ed. C. F. BUHLER, EETS, 1941, 44.
19 *Ibid.*, 333, n. 44.
20 *The Prologues and Epilogues of William Caxton*, ed. W. J. B. CROTCH, EETS, 1928, 70.

21 E. VINAVER, ed. *The Works of Sir Thomas Malory*, Oxford, 1954, 882.
22 *Pecock, The Folower to the Donet*, ed. E. V. HITCHCOCK, EETS, 1924, 151.
23 *Ibid.*, 138.
24 *The Earliest English Translation of the ... De Imitatione Christi*, ed. J. K. INGRAM, EETS, 1893, xxv.

Part three The Renaissance

Chapter 7

The Impact of Humanist Latinity

The movement that began in Florence in the late fourteenth century spread quickly through western Europe and began to affect England by the end of the fifteenth century. For those scholars and men of letters who were in the movement it was a world new-minted, the rebirth of learning, the renaissance; the dark ages were past. Recent scholarship looks more cautiously at this self-advertising concept of a renaissance. There had been several great periods in the Middle Ages when learning was equally alive and great art was being executed. Good English prose had been established for centuries. Nevertheless, something new and important did happen in Europe in the fifteenth and sixteenth centuries. The rediscovery of the classical past, the unearthing and printing of the full texts of Latin and Greek authors unknown to the mediaeval reader, produced a rising excitement. Doors were opening on to a different world. The key lay, not in the mediaeval Latin of Christian writers, but in the secular and more 'human' literature, the *literae humaniores*, of ancient Greece and Rome. The fashionable medium for the new humanist writers became classical Latin as exemplified by Cicero and codified by the Latin rhetorician Quintilian.

The trend of political history played into the hands of the humanists. Secular power in mediaeval Europe had been dispersed among innumerable landed magnates. The fifteenth and sixteenth centuries saw the rise of the Prince, the consolidation of central monarchies. The Prince required an efficient and literate civil service and able diplomats for his negotiations. Humanist scholars of every country, writing and speaking the 'same language', the new Latinity, filled the bill admirably. In England, where humanism was slow off the mark, Henry the Seventh found he had to import his scholars from Europe.

The result in England was a new kind of education for a new kind of scholar. Church Latin for the priest and English for the lesser gentry and the burgher was no longer adequate. The young man of good family, if he were to administer his own estates, or engage at court or abroad in the King's business, had to be apprenticed to the new learning. Schools and universities did not change overnight. Much of the mediaeval curriculum remained for a time, though with a change of emphasis towards rhetoric. New school text-books, like Whittinton's *Vulgaria* (1520), were written to replace the older Donatus. Humanist educational ideas, inspired often by renaissance Italian court-educators, established the pattern of the English grammar school. The universities began to teach Greek, and the new 'pure' Latin. By the middle of the sixteenth century humanist education had won a complete victory, its finest product not the learned priest but the educated nobleman. With some few but notable exceptions, authorship in the English renaissance is to become the preserve of the gentleman and the scholar.

The effect of all this on the writing of English prose was everywhere apparent. One should perhaps speak rather of the effects in the plural, for the influence of humanist Latinity, though it was widespread and permanent, did not tend all in the same direction. At one end of the scale a fine classical Latinist like Sir Thomas More wrote English prose of Anglo-Saxon simplicity; at the other extreme the chronicler Edward Hall and Sir Thomas Elyot introduced Latinisms as strange as the Saxonisms that Pecock had unsuccessfully tried to naturalise. Sir John Cheke, a vigorous propagandist for 'our own tung ... cleane and pure, unmixt and un-mangeled with borowing of other tunges',[1] wrote mainly in Latin; John Lyly's name is for ever linked with Euphuism, a balanced, antithetical, and un-Ciceronian manner of writing that yet owes everything to humanist Latinity. And throughout the sixteenth century a succession of writers ('translators' is hardly an adequate description of them) are moving steadily towards the unique combination of native simplicity and classical richness that makes up the English Bible.

This first century of the English Renaissance presents many facets. At the risk of some initial over-simplification, three major aspects of English prose, the Latin influence, the native tradition, and the prose of the Bible, will be dealt with in separate chapters. It is as well to remember that in all but a few doctrinaire writers, the strands are inextricably interwoven. Yet by identifying the separate elements, the pattern of prose of each individual author becomes clearer.

The sixteenth-century educated Englishman wrote Ciceronian Latin, often with some elegance, conscious of a European audience. His attitude to English prose was equivocal. His training had implanted in him an admiration for Latin as the language of intelligent communication. His instincts and his national feeling (particularly after the Reformation) induced him to defend the writing of prose in English. What can only be described as a sham battle developed in the first three-quarters of the century; it was to continue in the next as the equally sham Battle of the Books. Was English a language in which intelligent men could write? On the one side were ranged men like Edward Hall, Sir Thomas Elyot, and the early writers of Rhetorics, for whom English lacked the 'eloquence' of Ciceronian Latin. English in such writers is characterised as 'rude', 'plain cloth' (as opposed to the 'Roman velvet'), 'barbarous'.[2] It lacked the vocabulary for abstract ideas and the 'colours' of renaissance rhetoric. On the other side were Sir Thomas More and his circle, quietly accepting for writing the English prose they spoke, and the controversialists like Sir John Cheke and his circle, which included Roger Ascham and Sir Thomas Wilson, who damned the Latin neologisms, the 'inkhorn terms' and 'indenture English' of the opposition, and found their own language 'adequate' and even 'plentiful'. The battle had really been won long before. What R. F. Jones calls the renaissance 'triumph of the English language' had in fact taken place two centuries earlier. The most significant feature of the sixteenth-century controversy on the adequacy of English as a language for written prose was that both sides conducted the affair in English. They did not differ on the real essential, that prose could and should continue to be written in their own language.

Humanist Latinity has left its most abiding mark on English in the enormous expansion of vocabulary that took place in the sixteenth century. Thousands of Latin words were adapted into English to meet the needs of religious and political discussion and the far-ranging expansion of ideas that was a feature of the whole European renaissance. Cheke as a purist ranged himself with Pecock: in his translation of St. Matthew he preferred 'crossed' to 'crucified', 'forsayers' to 'prophets', and 'hundreder' to 'centurion'. His followers, even while they echoed his attack on inkhorn words, were more accommodating: Wilson in *The Arte of Rhetorique* (1553) agreed that where Latin or Greek words were admitted into English 'either for lacke of store, or els because we would enrich the language: it is well doen to use them'.

It is of some significance that the most outrageous ink-horn terms of the period generally occur in parodies and examples cited contemptuously by the purist group. Wilson attacks the trend to 'catche an ynke horne terme by the taile'. He illustrates it not from a real author but from a 'Lincolneshire man' applying for a benefice:

I doubt not but you will adiuuate such poore adnichilate orphanes, as whilome ware condisciples with you, and of antique familiaritie in

Lincolneshire. Among whom I being a Scholasticall panion, obtestate your Sublimitie, to extoll mine infirmitie. There is a Sacerdotall dignitie in my natiue Countrey contiguate to me, where I now contemplate ...[3]

[*The Arte of Rhetorique*]

The real ink-horn men (as opposed to such imaginary bogies) were of two types. First there were the decorators, writing an 'aureate' diction on anxious tip-toe. Skelton, though a vigorous colloquial poet, writes in aureate prose (with no suspicion of parody):

Yong scolers ... whan they haue delectably lycked a lytell of the lycorous electuary of lusty lernyng, in the moche studious scolehous of scrupulous Philology ... were puffed so full of vaynglorious pompe and surcudant elacyon ...[4]

[*A Replycacion*, 1528]

Edward Hall began his 1542 *Chronicle* with 'what mischiefe hath insurged in realmes by intestine devision' and clearly laid himself open to the contemporary charge of 'indenture' English. These latinising decorators did little harm. Their eccentricities were rejected. Many of their words have remained. Their more pedantic aberrations were to provide Shakespeare with his schoolmaster Holofernes, presenting an entertainment 'in the posterior of this day', and his companion, the curate Nathaniel, with his request to 'abrogate scurrility'.

Contributors of more permanence were those serious authors who wrestled with the 'inadequacy' of English. Of these the most important was Sir Thomas Elyot. His linguistic interest led him to produce a *Latin-English Dictionary* in 1538. His practice is seen in his manual on the education of the renaissance aristocrat, *The Boke named The Governour*, 1531. Throughout the book he finds himself faced with the lack of suitable vocabulary for ideas 'where unto we lacke a name in englisshe'. He is thereby 'constrained to usurpe a latine worde for the necessary augmentation of our language'. Elyot's augmentations may have been ink-horn to the opposition. His linguistic tact was such that (unlike the decorators') much of his latinised vocabulary has survived. We could not do without the many words (e.g. *modesty, mediocrity, industrious, frugality, beneficence*) for which the NED can find no earlier record than in *The Governor*.

Humanist Latinity so set a permanent mark on the vocabulary of English prose. The result was not merely to increase the range of words available. The new polysyllabic Latin words affected the movement of the sentence.

Once they had settled down into their final English form, they had to be matched in with the shorter and structural native words. The early experiments were naturally not always successful. Once balance was achieved, the result was an expanded prose rhythm, the over-riding movement of natural speech supplemented by the lesser rhythms of Latinised nouns and verbs, which culminated at the end of the century in Hooker and in the great preachers of the seventeenth century. But before this new formal prose of the great public occasion could come into being, humanist Latinity had further work to do.

Up till the end of the fifteenth century the paratactic or co-ordinate native sentence-structures had continued to produce the best prose. The cumulative trailing sentence copied from mediaeval French had proved a poorer model. It was inevitable that a new generation brought up to reproduce the Ciceronian period should look afresh at the sentence-structure of their own language. The classical Latin sentence, with its subordination (hypotaxis) of clauses, its massive but controlled length, its delayed verb, its sense not completed till the last word had been written, its skilful intricacy and artful, rhythmical devices, was a challenge to renaissance virtuosity, and it was speedily imitated so far as (and sometimes beyond what) the mechanics of the English sentence would permit. Many renaissance writers attempted these lengthy and complex sentences; a couple of examples, one earlier, one later in the century, will suffice:

> Amonge the romanes, Caius Julius Cesar, whiche firste toke upon him the perpetuall rule and gouernaunce of the empire, is a noble example of industrie, for in his incomparable warres and busynesse incredible (if the autoritie and faithe of the writers were nat of longe tyme approued) he dyd nat onely excogitate moste excellent policies and deuises to vainquisshe or subdue his enemies, but also prosecuted them with suche celeritie and effecte, that diuers and many tymes he was in the campe of his enemies, or at the gates of their townes or fortresses, whan they supposed that he and his hoste had ben two days iournay from thens, leauing to them no tyme or layser to consulte or prepare agayne hym sufficient resistence.[5]
>
> [ELYOT, *The Governor*, 1531]

Thomas North, who produced his 'Plutarch', the *Lives of the Noble Grecians and Romans* in 1579, comes too late to be regarded as an experimenter. He writes with idiomatic assurance, although he is working from the French of Amyot. Yet the movement of Latin, not Anglo-Saxon, controls such a sentence as the following:

Who when he was returned unto his campe, his souldiers came in great companies unto him, and were very sory, that he mistrusted he was not able with them alone to overcome his enemies, but would put his person in daunger, to goe fetch them that were absent, putting no trust in them that were present.[6]

[*Life of Caesar*]

This is the 'periodic' sentence, which by the nineteenth century came to be regarded by English grammar writers as the ultimate form of good prose. Its use (and its usefulness) was both in the sixteenth century and later limited. It required a subject worthy of its weight. Unless it was supported by rhetorical devices to signal what was important, the subordinate clauses beat on the ear in monotonous succession, each demanding the same degree of attention. Where (as in the Elyot sentence) a parenthesis carried as much weight as the main statement, mere syntactical subordination was insufficient to hold down to its proper level a clause of lesser semantic importance. Directly copying the structure of the Latin sentence was inadequate, as can be seen from a later example from Milton:

Julius Caesar (of whom, and of the Roman Free State, more than what appertains, is not here to be discours'd) having subdu'd most parts of Gallia, which by a potent faction, he had obtain'd of the Senat as his province for many years, stirr'd up with a desire of adding still more glory to his name, and the whole Roman Empire to his ambition, som say, with a farr meaner and ignobler, the desire of Brittish Pearls, whose bigness he delighted to balance in his hand, determins, and that upon no unjust pretended occasion, to trie his Force in the conquest also of Britain.[7]

[*History of Britain*, 1670]

Here, after a century and a half of humanist influence, is a sentence (from a writer who could write great prose) which is simply not English. The late position of the main verb, the jungle of parentheses and subordinate clauses would do very well in Latin, which has its own signalling devices for what is more and what is less semantically important. If English writers were to abandon their native parataxis and co-ordination in an effort to rival the complexity of a Ciceronian sentence something more than Latin structure was required.

The answer lay in Quintilian, the Roman writer on rhetoric, whose *Institutio Oratoria* had been discovered in a complete text by the Italian humanist Poggio in 1416, the first printed edition appearing in 1470. It led to a series of Rhetorics in English. The earliest, Cox's *Rhetoric* (1524) was followed by Sherry's *Schemes and Tropes* (1550), Wilson's *The Arte of Rhetorique* (1553), and thereafter by a succession of Elizabethan handbooks. Wilson was undoubtedly the most influential, his treatise running into many editions.

Book three of *The Arte of Rhetorique* is a manual on the technique of writing 'rhetorical' prose, divided into four headings: plainness; aptness; composition; exornation. Plainness and aptness are the recommended qualities for the individual word. Thereafter, 'when we have learned usuall and accustomable words to set forth our meaning', we are ready to learn composition, defined as 'an apt ioyning together of wordes in such order, that neither the eare shall espie any ierre [jar] nor yet any man shalbe dulled with overlong drawing out of a sentence, nor yet much confounded with mingling of causes such as are needelesse, being heaped together without reason, and used without number'. The trailing fifteenth-century 'French' sentence and the clumsier Ciceronian efforts could hardly be more appropriately described. Wilson then explains the various types of exornation, the figures of speech and 'colours of rhetoric' with which to 'beautifie our talke with divers goodly colours ... that our speech may seeme as bright and precious, as a rich stone is faire and orient'.

From Quintilian and his English exponents (plus, it must not be forgotten, their inheritance of normal speech patterns) the Elizabethans at the end of the century learned one of their major prose styles. Wilson had preached the renaissance doctrine of decorum: the prose must fit the subject and the level at which it is written. Words and sentence pattern must be 'apt and agreeable'. These may vary from the condensed native maxim like 'Enough is as good as a feast' (he recommends Heywood's proverbs which had recently appeared in print) to the elaborate or 'exornated' sentences adorned with all the 'colours of rhetoric'. Exornation opened the way – and Wilson provided full examples – for new sentence-structures with 'egall members' (the balanced antithetical sentence), 'gradation' and 'progression' (the paratactic cumulation of short main clauses leading to a climax), 'contrarietie' (antithesis of opposites, as in 'To his friend he is churlish, to his foe he is gentle'), the series of sentences with 'like endings' or with 'repetition' (like opening words), plus the verbal metaphors, the longer 'similitudes', and the whole gallery of 'tropes', 'schemes', and 'figures of speech' of the last few decades of the sixteenth century.

The lesson taught, the pupils were apt. There were many individual differences between the euphuism of the early Lyly (*Euphues*, 1578) and the prose of his plays, between Sidney's *Arcadia* (1577–80) and the romances of slightly later date like Green's *Pandosto* (1588) and Lodge's *Rosalind*

(1590) or Pettie, the earlier pioneer in the style (*A Petite Pallace of Pettie his Pleasure*, 1576). To approach them from the prose of the earlier humanists is to recognise that this new generation are essentially alike. They have absorbed humanist Latinity and read their rhetorics. The ink-horn battle is over and a delight in words is legitimate. The imagination is licensed to soar on the wings of metaphor, and the new sentence-patterns challenge their ingenuity. They are writing romances – the point is worth stressing – for women of leisure, who knew no Latin and could not recognise a Ciceronian sentence, but who were prepared to be dazzled by a display of English rhetoric.

So in one sentence of Pettie we find Wilson's figures of 'short sentences' and 'like among themselves' followed by 'contrary things repeated together':

> Then must their maids be monied, their bawds bribed, their scouts considered, their servants satisfied, and ever as they lie open to him so his purse must lie open to them and theirs.[8]
>
> [Pallace of Pleasure, 1576, mod. sp.]

Lyly can combine Wilson's figures of 'egall members', 'contrarietie', 'asking other, and aunswering our selfe', 'rejection', 'similitude', and 'like among themselves' all within a few sentences:

> O my *Euphues*, would I had thy wit, or thou my wil. Shal I utter this to thee, but thou art more likely to correct my follyes with counsaile, than to comfort me with any pretie conceit. Thou wilt say that she is a Lady of great credit, and I heere of no countenaunce. I but *Euphues*, low trees haue their tops, smal sparkes their heat, the Flye his splene, the Ant hir gall, *Philautus* his affection, which is neither ruled by reason, nor led by appointment.[9]
>
> [Euphues and his England, 1580]

The Euphuists are, of course, showing off, like boys who have just learned to ride a bicycle. Sidney does not need to show off. Humanist rhetoric is second nature to him:

> Therefore mourne boldly, my Inke; for while she lookes upon you, your blacknes wil shine: crie out boldly, my Lamentation; for while she reads you, your cries will be musicke. Say then (O happy messenger of a most unhappy message) that the too soone borne, too late dying creature, which dares not speake, no not looke, no not scarcely thinke (as from his miserable selfe, unto her heavenly highnesse) onely

presumes to desire thee (in the time that her eyes and voice doo exalt thee) to say, and in this manner to say, not from him, O no, that were not fit, but of him.[10]

[*Arcadia*, written c. 1580]

Unlike the Ciceronian sentence (which for most purposes wound to a halt in the seventeenth century), the new varieties of sentence induced by humanist rhetoric were in the language for good. Authors as diverse as Dr. Johnson, Oscar Wilde, and G. B. Shaw re-echo the patterns in later centuries.

The two best humanist prose-writers of the sixteenth century, Cranmer and Hooker, merit individual consideration. To say that their English is based on Latin is true, but it is no more than a partial explanation of their achievement. They alone of the Latinists of the century not only matched but outshone their originals.

Cranmer's *Book of Common Prayer* (1549), though it glances at earlier English devotional books, is mainly a translation of the mediaeval Latin service, the *Sarum Use* of Salisbury. The Latin of the *Sarum Use*, mediaeval and not classical, is a perfect medium for its purpose. The rhythms (or cursus) are carefully worked out for effective oral delivery. In particular the prayers or *orationes* (from which the *Book of Common Prayer* derived its collects) are Latin periodic sentences of astonishing virtuosity. Cranmer was a Protestant, but he had no intention of giving up a liturgy centuries old. His problem – triumphantly solved – was to create an English prose for oral delivery which would match the Latin in dignity, rhythm and resonance. Create is perhaps the wrong word. As a preacher he could not but be instinctively aware of the continuing tradition of English spoken religious prose. What he did can best be judged by setting the Latin along-side his English rendering of one of the collects (for the fourth Sunday after Epiphany):

Deus qui nos in tantis periculis constitutos pro humana scis fragilitate non posse subsistere, da nobis salutem mentis et corporis ut ea quae pro peccatis nostris patimur te adiuvante vincamus.

One problem was the Latin verbs. They carry a heavier semantic load than was common in sixteenth-century English. A further problem was the Latin sentence-structure: three of the carefully subordinated phrases in the Latin are embedded in non-finite verbal constructions – a participle (*con-stitutos*), an accusative and infinitive (*nos ... non posse*), and an ablative absolute (*te adiuvante*). None of these (*pace* the Ciceronians) are possible English constructions. Cranmer solves his problems with idiomatic ease:

> God, whiche knowest us to bee set in the middest of so many and great daungers, that for mannes fraylnes we cannot alwayes stande uprightly; Graunt to us the health of body and soule that al those thinges which we suffer for sinne, by thy helpe we may wel passe and overcome.

Constitutos has been rendered by the monosyllabic 'to bee set'; to offset the loss of the polysyllabic Latin word, he expands *tantis* into 'so many and great'. The accusative and infinitive becomes a full English clause, the semantic force of the Latin verb *subsistere* now carried by the adverb 'uprightly'. *Te adiuvante* is reduced to a prepositional phrase 'by thy helpe'; and again to offset the loss of the longer Latin phrase and to match the Latin final rhythm of *te adiuvante vincamus*, he expands the verb *vincamus* into the fuller English rhythm of 'we may wel passe and overcome'. *Mentis et corporis* he turns to the traditional English order of 'body and soule'. The final form of the collect moves to a formal and resonant rhythm that is nonetheless firmly based on the stresses of informal spoken English.

Hooker comes at the very end of the first century of humanism. His *Laws of Ecclesiastical Polity* was published in 1593–7. After almost a century of polemic characterised by colloquial and even street-corner invective, Hooker defends the position of the Anglican Church in a philosophical work great both in content and in prose style. A couple of sentences he wrote in defence of the service of his Church could equally describe his concept of the writing of prose:

> We somewhat the rather incline to length, lest over-quick dispatch of a duty so important should give the world occasion to deem that the thing itself is but little accounted of, wherein but little time is bestowed. Length thereof is a thing which the gravity and weight of such actions doth require.[11]

The long periodic sentence is his staple, but it is Hooker, not Cicero, who is in command. The varying levels of emphasis (something the earlier Ciceronians could not bring about) are reinforced to the appropriate degree by rhetorical devices. However long Hooker's sentence may be, we are never lost, never in doubt as to his major statement. One of his commonest sentence-structures consists of a series of subordinate clauses with 'like beginnings' followed by a resounding conclusion. The often-quoted anthology passage beginning 'Now if nature should intermit her course' [*Ecclesiastical Polity*, Book I, iii, 2] is a two-hundred-word sentence consisting of a series of 'if' clauses (most of them containing further sub-subordinate clauses), all in a highly Latinised vocabulary ('irregular volubility') leading up to the almost monosyllabic finale: 'What would become of man himself, whom these things now do all serve?'[12] Hooker knows the value of native parataxis: a three-hundred-word sentence on prayer [Book V, xxvii, 1] can be analysed into a series of paratactic sub-statements with 'like beginnings': 'It hath ... it differeth ... it requireth ... it intermingleth ... it appointeth ... it spendeth ...' and just before the moment when the series might become artificially repetitive, he switches skilfully to a different final construction.[13] Balance, antithesis, chiasmus, metaphor, and the other colours of rhetoric, which in lesser writers is euphuism, in Hooker is an unobtrusive reinforcement of his meaning:

> Where Rome keepeth that which is ancienter and better, others whom we much more affect leaving it for newer and changing it for worse; we had rather follow the perfections of them whom we like not, than in defects resemble them whom we love.[14]

The secret of Hooker and Cranmer lay in their feeling for the movement of English speech. Humanist Latinity and renaissance rhetoric give them an expanded sentence; the ultimate shape of their every phrase follows the normal spoken rhythm. The alliteration ('pardon and peace', 'the mother of such magnificence') and the words in pairs ('we have erred and strayed', 'increase and multiply') go back a long way in English. It is the great achievement of these two that they unite what humanism had to offer with the natural continuity of the native tradition, the theme of the ensuing chapter.

Notes

1 *The Book of the Courtier*, 'Cheke's Letter to Thomas Hoby', Everyman edition, 7.
2 R. F. JONES, *The Triumph of the English Language*, Stanford, 1953, Ch. 1.
3 G. H. MAIR, ed., *Wilson's Arte of Rhetorique*, Oxford, 1909, 163.
4 J. DYCE, ed., *The Works of John Skelton*, London, 1843, i, 207–9.
5 THOMAS ELYOT, *The Governor*, Everyman edition, 1907, 100.
6 G. WYNDHAM, ed., *Plutarch's Lives by Sir Thomas North*, London, 1896, v, 41.
7 *The Works of John Milton*, Columbia edition, New York, 1932, x, 34.
8 I. GOLLANCZ, ed., *A Petite Pallace of Pettie his Pleasure*, London, 1908.
9 R. W. BOND, ed., *The Complete Works of John Lyly*, Oxford, 1902, ii, 90.

10 A. FEUILLERAT, ed., *Sidney's The Countess of Pembroke's Arcadia*, Cambridge, 1922, 181.
11 J. KEBLE, ed., *Hooker's Ecclesiastical Polity*, Oxford, 1888, ii, 145.
12 *Ibid.*, i, 207.
13 *Ibid.*, ii, 125.
14 *Ibid.*, ii, 127.

Chapter 8

The Native Continuity

While one group of humanist-trained writers in the sixteenth century was bent on reshaping the English sentence and augmenting the vocabulary of the language, another group was engaged in defending English as an adequate and even superior medium for prose: English was to the playwright Rastell in 1519 'sufficient', to the rhetorician Sherry in 1550 'plentiful', and to More as early as his *Utopia* of 1516 (though the quotation comes perforce from the translation of 1551) 'bothe copious in woordes and also pleasaunte to the eare, and for the utteraunce of a mans minde verye perfecte and sure'. Similar evidence can be readily gathered from the pages of Latimer, Cheke, Ascham, and Wilson in mid-century. By the last quarter of the century the single defending voices have merged into a chorus of praise, led by Sidney ('our language ... beeing indeed capable of any excellent exercising of it')[1] and the Epistle Dedicatory to the Shepheards Calendar ('Our Mother tonge, which truely of itself is both ful enough for prose and stately enough for verse').

These writers were all, like the previous group, humanist trained, brought up, like them, on Ciceronian Latin. But when they defend and praise their 'mother tongue', they are not thinking of the prose that was to culminate in Cranmer and in Hooker. It is clear both from their critical utterances and from their own practice that the 'mother tongue' is their inherited spoken English. When they wrote, their intention was (in the words of the editor of *The Arte of Rhetorique*) to write as men spoke; to use no words and no constructions not already familiar to all their readers.[2] There was nothing new in this. It had been the normal practice in Anglo-Saxon and Middle English and in what I have called the 'spoken' prose of the fifteenth century. What was new was the status of the men who chose to write in this manner. They were not mediaeval clerics writing for women; they were not Paston squires or middle-class brewers setting down their own language because they knew no other. They were humanists, diplomats, university dons, noblemen, graduates and Inns of

Court men. A fair proportion of them were familiar with life in the royal palaces.

This being so, R. W. Chambers' views on the 'continuity of English prose' call for some modification. Continuity there undoubtedly was; but it is impossible to confine it, as he does, to the homiletic tradition reappearing in Sir Thomas More and the translations of the Bible.[3] More, indeed, wrote more controversy than religious meditation. His writing has often affinity with the *Merry Tales* rather than with the *Ancrene Riwle*. The prose of the Bible (the discussion belongs to the following chapter) has always been a thing apart. The real continuity depended on speech, and secular speech at that. More is a great writer of prose, but he is part of the general movement of his century, one of these periods of adjustment when the writing of English moved once again closer to the spoken tongue. The resemblance of the sixteenth-century sermon, the Elizabethan cony-catching pamphlet, and the broadsides of religious controversy is not accidental. They were addressed to the same audience, by educated men seeking to make contact with a whole nation.

The sixteenth-century sermon (massively collected in the volumes of the Parker Society) survives as a close transcript of what was originally spoken. The Protestant clerics of the time were seldom concerned with literary ostentation or verbal arabesques. Sermon merges into polemic as the preacher sets down in plain language and colloquial structures the claims of the new religion. The urgency of winning over a total population in a religious battle was more important than describing the joys of heaven or the torments of hell. The result is a brisk and pungent short sentence with the cut and thrust of debate:

> If ever it should happen to you to be present again at the mass, think but thus with yourselves: What make I here? What profit have I of my doings? I hear nothing; I understand nothing; I am taught nothing; I receive nothing; Christ bade me take; I take nothing; Christ bade me eat; I eat nothing; Christ bade me drink; I drink nothing. Is this the institution of Christ? Is this the Lord's supper?[4]
>
> [JOHN JEWEL, *Sermon at Paul's Cross*, 1560]

Jewell, who had earlier written a treatise against rhetoric, in the same sermon enunciates clearly his principles of communication:

> First, as touching the unknown and strange tongue that hath been used in the mass, St. Paul's counsel and commandment is in general, that whatsoever is done or said in the congregation should be so done

and said that the hearers may have comfort thereby, and yield thanks to God, and say, Amen.[5]

Hugh Latimer emerges from the period as the best prose-writer of the sermon. His homely imagery and controlled colloquial speech are seen at their best in the well-known *Sermon of the Plough* of 1548. In all his writing he has a remarkable feeling for the native sentence-structure:

> There is a common saying amongst us here in England, 'Every thing is, say they, as it is taken;' which indeed is not so: for every thing is as it is, howsoever it is taken.[6]
>
> [*Sermon at Grimsthorpe*, 1553]

In such a sentence Latimer exploits beautifully the native sentence-structure. The meaning is carried by the syntax; the verbs, in particular, work at full capacity. The same sermon ends with a fine passage of Latimer at his best. The tone is that of intimate but not vulgar conversation, in which the key-word 'stick' is exactly right in the context:

> I have troubled you a good while, and somewhat the longer, because I had much pleasure to comfort myself in it. In times past we were wont to run hither and thither, to this saint and to that saint; but it is all but fig-leaves what man can do. Let us therefore stick to Christ, which is the right, perfect, and absolute Saviour, and able to deliver us from all our sins; and not only able to do it, but also willing.[7]

This is the prevailing tone of the sixteenth-century sermon. The Church set its seal on the style by the official issue in 1547 of *Certeyne Sermons, or Homelies appoynted by the Kynges Maiestie to be declared and redde*, which included Latimer, among other accepted preachers. A second series, edited by Jewell, was published in 1562–3. Both volumes were constantly reprinted. This direct, colloquial and unrhetorical writing remained the approved sermon style till the end of the century:

> The flesh sayth, Soule, take thine ease, eate, drinke, and goe brave, lye soft, what else should you doe but take your pleasure? Thou knowest what a pleasant fellowe I have beene unto thee ...[8]

This relaxed conversational manner, with its 'ungrammatical' but idiomatic shift from 'thou' to 'you', its imagery so close to that of Greene and Dekker, comes from the 1592 collected sermons of Henry Smith, whom Thomas Fuller (turning aside from his own later age of resounding pulpit eloquence) was to call 'silver-tongued Smith'. The phrase had been used of Smith by Thomas Nashe in 1592. Its persistence shows the continuing approbation of this sixteenth-century sermon style.

The public events of the century made it inevitable that Protestant writing of this type would predominate in print. But in the battle for men's minds the Catholic writers were equally seized of the necessity for communication at the level of the audience they hoped to retain, the common man. When in the 1620's copies of the reformer Tyndale's English translation of the New Testament began to appear in England, the Bishop of London turned for assistance not to a Ciceronian or a rhetoric-writer but to the man whom he could trust to write the English that men would understand. *Frater clarissime in lingua nostra vernacula*, he wrote to Sir Thomas More in 1527, calling on him to refute the new heresies. More responded with his *Dialogue* against Tyndale of 1528. Their doctrines differ, but the movement of his prose is that of John Jewel's, co-ordinate main statements matched by rhetorical questions:

> In some countryes thei go on hunting comonly on good friday in the morninge for a comon custome. Wyll ye breke that evyll custome or, cast away good friday? There be cathedrall churches unto which the countre commeth with procession at whytsuntyde and the women folowing the crosse wyth many an unwomanly songe, and that such honest wyves as out of the procession ye could not heare to speke one such foule rybaudrie worde as thei there synge for gods sake hole ribaudous songes, as lowd as theyr throte can cry. Wil ye mend that lewde manner, or put away whytsontide?[9]

More, one might argue, is merely matching Tyndale, who can wield a blunt instrument with equal skill:

> As soon as the monks were fallen, then sprang these begging friars out of hell, the last kind of caterpillars, in a more vile apparel, and a more strait religion; that, if aught of relief were left among the laymen for the poor people, these horse-leeches might suck that also.[10]
>
> [TYNDALE: *The Practice of Prelates*, 1530]

> And when thou stickest up a candle before the image, thou mightest with as good reason make a hollow belly in the image, and pour in meat and drink: for as the saint neither eateth nor drinketh, so hath he no bodily eyes to delight in the light of a candle.[11]
>
> [TYNDALE: *An Answer to Sir Thomas More's Dialogue*, 1531]

But More had been chosen as spokesman, not so much for his skill in controversy as for his written command of the spoken tongue. As early as 1513 he had in his *History of Richard III* shown his mastery of native sentence-structure and vocabulary:

> And thereuppon by and by after the messenger departed, hee caused in all haste al his servauntes to be called uppe, and so with his owne householde aboute hym, and everie manne weaponed, hee tooke the greate Seale with him, and came yet beefore daye unto the Queene. About whome he found much heavinesse, rumble, haste, and businesse, carriage and conveyaunce of her stuffe into Sainctuary, chestes, coffers, packes, fardelles, trusses, all on mennes backes, no man unoccupyed, somme lading, somme goynge, somme descharging, somme commynge for more, somme breakinge downe the walles to bring in the nexte waye, and somme yet drewe to them that holpe to carrye a wronge waye.[12]

It is no wonder that More found English prose (with no overlay of Latin sentence-structure or vocabulary) 'bothe copious in woordes ... and for the utteraunce of a mans minde verye perfecte and sure'.

This is still his basic style when he turns to religious meditation, as he did on several occasions, but nowhere more memorably than when (awaiting death in the Tower) he wrote in 1534 his great *Dialogue of Comfort Against Tribulation*. There are magnificent chapters, notably that on Christ's passion (Book iii, Ch. 27) and that on 'the unsurety of lands and possessions':

> What great difference is that to us whether our substance be moveable or unmoveable, sith we be so moveable ourself, that we may be removed from them both, and lose them both twain ... Who ought your castle, cousin, three thousand years ago?[13]

This is but the basic style turned to a graver topic. Elsewhere in the book, in his 'merry tales', his colloquial phrases like 'crick in the back', 'cock-a-hoop', 'up a cop', and his Christ who 'clucketh home unto him even those chickens of his that wilfully walk abroad', there is the essential prose of More, who wrote not to dazzle but to be understood. More's influence in his own day was considerable. He was the centre of a literary circle which included John Rastell and William Roper, who was to repay his debt in his magnificent life of his martyred father-in-law. Echoes of his style, though hardly of his greatness, still linger on in the prose of Catholic recusant writers to the end of the century.[14]

The second centre of native prose was, on the face of it, more surprising.

But St. John's College, Cambridge, became early in the century a focal point for renaissance humanism and the reformed religion, a blend that often resulted in a passion for plainness. Sir John Cheke – he tutored the future Queen Elizabeth, who could certainly speak and write bluntly – was the leader of the movement and (as has been indicated in the last chapter) a doctrinaire extremist for 'clean and pure' English prose. His views are summed up in the letter he wrote in 1557 as an introduction to Hoby's translation of Castiglione's *Courtier*. More moderate – and more effective – were his friends Sir Thomas Wilson, whose *Arte of Rhetorique* made 'plainnesse and aptnesse' the first criteria of good writing, and Roger Ascham, a Fellow of St. John's, and like Cheke a tutor to Elizabeth.

Ascham's *Toxophilus* (1545), on the art of shooting with the long bow, is 'written in the Englishe tongue, for Englishe men'. What Ascham means by English he makes clear in his preface 'To all gentel men and yomen of England':

> He that wyll wryte well in any tongue, muste folowe thys councel of Aristotle, to speake as the common people do, to thinke as wise men do.[15]

Toxophilus is primarily a work of technical exposition, in the colloquial style now well established for that genre; but it is much more, a eulogy of English manners and the English countryside (it has one of the finest descriptions of a snowy landscape ever written), done in an admirably direct and lively prose. Good clean shooting and good clean English prose were for Ascham moral necessities. It is easy to see in this book the genesis of his *The Schoolmaster*, published after his death in 1570, with its insistence on 'plaine naturall English'. From there it is a short step – little more than ten years – to Mulcaster, Spenser's schoolmaster, who in his *Elementarie* (1582) advocated the use of English, 'the naturall tung', in the schools since:

> This *prerogative* and libertie, which the peple hath to use bothe speche and pen at will, is the cause and yet not blamed therefor why the English writers be now finer then theie were some hundreth yeares ago.[16]

The collocation of 'speech and pen' is significant. To Mulcaster they used the same medium.

Mulcaster wrote these words a year or so after the publication of *Euphues*. This fashionable success notwithstanding, it was the 'naturall tung' and not the 'colours of rhetoric' which produced the most distinctively Elizabethan prose, the astonishing virtuosity of the pamphlet. The pamphlet began, as did so much in the century, in religious dissension. Though there are earlier examples, what sparked off the great age of prose-pamphleteering was the Marprelate controversy of 1588-9. 'Martin Marprelate', an anonymous puritan, attacked the Anglican government of the Church in a series of bluntly colloquial tracts:

> I knowe I am misliked of many which are your enemies, that is of many which you cal Puritans. It is their weaknes; I am threatened to be hanged by you. What though I were hanged; do you thinke your cause shalbe the better? For the day that you hange Martin assure your selves there wil 20 Martins spring in my place. I meane not now, you grosse beastes ...[17]

The Bishops had to answer, quickly, and in the same idiom. Had not More been a match for Tyndale? They turned to a group of young writers, all university men, all humanist trained, all up till then writers of exclusively rhetorical prose, Lyly, Robert Greene, and Thomas Nashe. For the author of *Euphues* the writing of the colloquial *Pappe with a Hatchet* of 1589 was evidently merely an exercise. But for Greene and Nashe the writing of pamphlets of religious controversy was a turning-point. Both (the point is significant) had been educated at St. John's College, Cambridge, the college of Cheke and Ascham. They were aware of the tradition in which they had to write: Nashe in his 1592 *Pierce Penilesse his Supplication* praised More, Ascham and Cheke among 'the chiefe pillers of our english speech'.[18] The flurry of invective against Martin lasted little more than a year. When it was over Greene and Nashe had found their prose style and their metier, the journalistic description and commentary on Elizabethan life in a richly colloquial prose that has seldom been equalled.

Greene's reputation as a prose writer rests on his 'cony-catching' pamphlets of 1591-2. They form a brilliant series of exposures of Elizabethan low-life, where the innocent are robbed by the vicious, the 'poore conies robbed by these base-minded caterpillers'. He draws on resources of the English language that had barely been touched, and certainly not by a literary man of his background. Canting phrases and thieves' slang rub shoulders with the proverbial maxims that had already gained the approval of *The Arte of Rhetorique*. The sentence-structure and sentence-links are exclusively those of spoken English:

> I am but an ignorant man at cards, and I see you have them at your

fingers end, I will play with you at a game wherein can be no deceit, it is called mum-chance at cardes, and it is thus: you shall shuffle the cards, and I will cut, you shal cal one, and this honest countrie yoman shal call a card for me, and which of our cards comes first shal win: here you see is no deceit, and this Ile play.[19]

[*A Notable Discovery of Coosnage*, 1591]

But this is not a 'tape-recording' of ordinary speech. It is a skilful *literary* reconstitution of conversation, based on speech movement. That Greene knew what he was doing is clear from *The Second Part of Conny Catching*, 1592, where he answers those critics who said he had no 'figures' and 'no eloquent phrases'. Greene defends his style in terms of the very rhetoric which is being adduced against him:

I reply that το πρεπον a certaine decorum is to bee kept in everie thing, and not to applie a high stile in a base subject.[20]

Nashe raised this colloquial style to concert pitch. Whether he is defending the Bishops in his Marprelate contributions or recreating the seven deadly sins (*Pierce Penilesse his Supplication*, 1592) or quarrelling with Gabriel Harvey (*Have with you to Saffron Walden*, 1596) or writing a mocking eulogy of Great Yarmouth (*Nashes Lenten Stuffe, or the Prayse of the Red Herring*, 1599) he adds to Greene's 'certaine decorum' a sheer inventiveness and fertility in phrase and language that is (the comparison is not impossible) Shakespearean:

As for the hindrance of Trades and Traders of the Citie by them [plays], that is an Article foysted in by the Vintners, Alewives, and Victuallers, who surmise if there were no Playes, they should have all the companie that resort to them, lye bowzing and beere-bathing in their houses every after-noone. Nor so, nor so, good brother bottle-ale, for there are other places besides where money can bestow it selfe: the signe of the smock will wipe your mouth cleane: and yet I have heard yee have made her a tenant to your tap-houses. But what shall hee doo that hath spent himselfe? Where shall hee haunt? Faith, when Dice, Lust, and Drunkennesse, and all have dealt upon him, if there be never a Playe for him to goe too for his pennie, he sits melancholie in his Chamber, devising upon felonie or treason, and howe he may best exalt himselfe by mischiefe.[21]

[*Pierce Penilesse his Supplication*, 1592]

Writing of this quality is common in Nashe. In him many of the movements of the Renaissance have come together to create alongside his contemporary Hooker, the second of the great Elizabethan prose styles. It has rhetoric, where required; it has colloquial strength and vigour and the continual movement of the speech sentence. But where Hooker went to Latin for decoration and richness, Nashe and his fellow pamphleteers turned to English and found (below-stairs as well as above) an abundance of vocabulary and phrase that had always been there but deemed unworthy of the printed page. Critics might grumble, or worse – Gabriel Harvey called Nashe's style 'an unsavory slaumpaump of wordes', paying him the unconscious tribute of imitation. By the 1590's the style was in, ousting rhetoric, steadily impressing itself on the drama, establishing a linguistic framework within which Elizabethan fiction could move from Arcadian romance to the new realism of Nashe's own *Unfortunate Traveller* (1593) and Deloney's *Jacke of Newbury* (1597). By the turn of the century Greene's defiant defence was unnecessary. Dekker after 1600 moves between the prose of the citizen comedy and the prose of the pamphlet with assurance. His plague pamphlets (1603 onwards), *The Seven Deadly Sins of London* (1606) and the *Gull's Hornbook* (1609) continue the Elizabethan theme of colloquial moralising on London life:

> The damask-coated Cittizen, that sat in his shop both forenoone and afternoone, and lookt more sowerly on his poore neighbours, then if he had drunke a quart of Vineger at a draught, sneakes out of his owne doores, and slips into a Taverne, where either alone, or with some other that battles their money together, they so plye themselves with penny pots, which (like small-shot) goe off, powring into their fat paunches, that at length they have not an eye to see withall, nor a good legge to stand upon. In which pickle if anye of them happen to be iustled downe by a post ...[22]
>
> [*The Seven Deadly Sins of London*, 1606]

It is a mistake to regard this as 'plain' prose, opposed to an 'ornate' latinised style. It is indeed a highly decorated prose, but the decoration consists in the literary exploitation of speech movement and the rediscovered resources of the full native vocabulary. It radiates metaphor and imagery at every turn.

Plain prose there was in considerable quantity. The technical manual and the neutral prose of exposition appear in hundreds of volumes. The most important topic for this study is literary criticism. The prose of the rhetorics and the growing body of Elizabethan criticism is, in general, workmanlike. It is readily accessible in Gregory Smith's volumes and need not be considered here in detail. A special and interesting example is

Sidney's *Defense of Poesy* written in the early 1580's. There are few traces of the 'rhetoric' of the *Arcadia*. Sidney, with his renaissance sense of decorum, fits his style to his topic and his genre. The tone and movement of the prose of the *Defense* is that of the 'naturall tung', the speech of an able but courteous debater. Sidney, in effect, is replying orally to Gosson's *Schoole of Abuse*, which had sparked off the controversy, In one sense, indeed, the *Defense* is a rather special example of the Elizabethan pamphlet.

Notes

1   C. GREGORY SMITH, ed., *Elizabethan Critical Essays*, Oxford, 1904, i, 204, 'An Apology for Poetry'.
2   G. H. MAIR, ed., *Wilson's Arte of Rhetorique*, Oxford, 1909, xxv.
3   R. W. CHAMBERS, 'Continuity of English Prose', *loc. cit.*
4   J. AYRE, ed., *The Works of John Jewel*, Parker Society, Cambridge, 1845, i, 25.
5   *Ibid.*, 8.
6   G. E. CORRIE, ed., *Sermons and Remains of Hugh Latimer*, Parker Society, Cambridge, 1845, 140.
7   *Ibid.*, 142.
8   HENRY SMITH, *Collected Sermons*, London, 1593.
9   W. E. CAMPBELL, ed., *The English Works of Sir Thomas More*, London, 1931, ii, 198.
10 H. WALTER, ed., *W. Tyndale, An Answer to Sir Thomas More*, Parker Society, Cambridge, 1849, 81.
11 H. WALTER, ed., *W. Tyndale, Expositions ... with the Practice of Prelates*, Parker Society, Cambridge, 1849, 277.
12 *English Works of Sir Thomas More, op. cit.*, i, 43.
13 SIR THOMAS MORE, *Utopia*, Everyman edition, 275-6, 'A Dyalogue of Comforte agaynste Tribulacyon', iii, 6.
14 A. C. SOUTHERN, *English Recusant Prose*, London, 1950, 3-13.
15 W. A. WRIGHT, ed., *The English Works of R. Ascham*, Cambridge, 1904, xiv.
16 K. J. HOLZKNECHT, ed., *Seventeenth Century Prose*, New York, 1954, 417: R. MULCASTER, 'The First Part of the Elementarie'.
17 HOLZKNECHT, *op. cit.*, 454: 'Hay Any Work for Cooper'.
18 R. B. MCKERROW, ed., *The Works of Thomas Nashe*, London, 1910, i, 194-5.
19 G. B. HARRISON, ed., *R. Greene's A Notable Discovery of Coosnage*, London, 1923, 27.
20 G. B. HARRISON, ed., *R. Greene's The Second and Last Part of Conny-Catching*, London, 1923, 7.
21 MCKERROW, *op. cit.*, i, 214.
22 H. F. B. BRETT-SMITH, ed., *T. Dekker's The Seven Deadly Sinnes of London*, Oxford, 1922, 31.

Chapter 9
The Prose of the Bible

The story of the successive translations of the Bible into English has been told many times and only a brief summary need be set down here, as a background for a discussion of the prose of the Scriptures. The Wycliffite versions of the fourteenth century, translated from the Latin of the Vulgate, had circulated in hundreds of manuscript copies, and these were available to the sixteenth-century translators, who take over occasional words and phrases. But the Bible as we know it began in the sixteenth century. Tyndale translated the New Testament (from the Greek text) and copies of his translation appeared in England by 1526. Before his death in 1536 he had completed (from the Hebrew) portions of the Old Testament, in particular the first five books, the Pentateuch. The first complete English Bible appeared in 1535; its translator, Miles Coverdale, leant heavily on Tyndale. Coverdale had not Tyndale's Greek and Hebrew scholarship, and his sources (apart from Tyndale) were the Vulgate and 'the Douche interpreters' (i.e. German translators). In 1537 a further translation by 'Thomas Matthew' (in fact, John Rogers) appeared, 'with the Kinges most gracyous lycence'. This officially approved Bible is substantially Tyndale's version supplemented by Coverdale's for those parts of the Old Testament which Tyndale had not translated. Being the first 'authorised version' it became the basis for subsequent official translations, with important consequences that will be considered later.

A further, officially sponsored, revision by Coverdale appeared in 1539 as the 'Great Bible'. This was reprinted in a second edition in 1540 with a preface by Cranmer, the title-page indicating that it was 'to be frequented and used in every churche'. The accession of Mary in 1553 put an end for some years to the public reading of Scripture. English Protestant scholars in exile produced in 1557–60 the Geneva Bible, which being available from the first edition as a small octavo remained for many years the most popular version for private reading. With the accession of Elizabeth the officially approved Great Bible and the uncomprisingly Protestant Geneva Bible were in a sense competitors, and Archbishop Parker resolved the situation by commissioning a further revision. He instructed his translators to 'follow the common English translation used in the churches'. This Bible, the Bishops' Bible of 1568, remained the Bible appointed to the use of churches until it was supplanted by the King James version of 1611.

Protestant activity in spreading the Scriptures in the common tongue finally evoked a reply from the unreformed Church. To the Catholics the Vulgate was the sacred text for which there could be no adequate English equivalent. But if the Protestants were gaining support with their mendacious renderings into English ('fraude ac mutatione sacrorum verborum') then an English version that satisfied Catholic theology must be produced. The New Testament appeared at Rheims in 1582 and the entire Catholic Bible was published at Douai 1609–10.[1]

This is merely an external history of some of the major translations. Throughout all the multiplicity of sixteenth-century versions of the Bible it is possible to see three clearly defined strands. First, and ultimately the most important, was the Tyndale translation, which was to provide the continuing basis for every officially approved version up to the Authorised of 1611. Secondly there were the more aggressively Protestant versions of which the Geneva Bible is the most important, written for the 'private reader' and characterised by the 'bitter notes' against which Parker warned his translators. Thirdly there was the heavily Latinate Rheims version, which retained many ecclesiastical words or phrases (e.g. 'Pasche', 'The feast of Azymes', 'The bread of Proposition') virtually unanglicised.[2] But every translator in the century leant on his predecessors. Even while their translations differed because of differences in theology (e.g. should ἐκκλησία be rendered as 'church' or as 'congregation'?) Protestant and Catholic and the differing levels of Protestantism borrowed silently from each other. In an age of humanistic scholarship no one hesitated to recognise (though he might not explicitly acknowledge) a bit of better scholarship, or even a more felicitous turn of words.

The prose of the Bible that was to become part of the fabric of English national life was established once and for all by Tyndale. Whatever the contributions of the rest, his choice of vocabulary and sentence-structure, even his choice of a starting-point (the New Testament, not the Old; the Gospels, not the Apocalypse) laid down the permanent pattern. It has been calculated that the Authorised Version retains some 90 per cent of Tyndale in the New Testament and in those portions of the Old Testament which he translated, but even where there is no Tyndale original the influence of his manner of writing is decisive.[3] The Bible is, of course, not a book but a literature, ranging from prose narrative through poetry to prophecy. Its foundation texts are partly in Hebrew, partly in Greek. Yet the general impression left by any extended reading of the English Bible is a basic unity of style. That unity was impressed by Tyndale.

Tyndale is a product of his age, a humanist scholar versed in Latin and deeply involved in the Hebrew and Greek of the new learning. Granted different interests, he might have become a Ciceronian, and an exponent of renaissance rhetoric. But the Lutheran currents of his time drove him elsewhere: the Scriptures had to be unlocked for the ordinary man – the 'boy that driveth the plough' – and the key was the vulgar tongue. Theoretically, Tyndale in the early sixteenth century had a choice of any of the current varieties of written English, the utilitarian 'spoken' style, Caxton-type translators' English, the latinised periodic (for which he could find some authority in the Vulgate), even early ink-horn. In fact, he had little choice. Partly by instinct, partly by early training ('the *English Chronicle*', he wrote in one of his Prefaces, 'I read when I was a child'),[4] and partly under the influences of his audience and his originals, he adopted that variety of the 'spoken' style which had been used since Alfred's day for the *Chronicle*:

> And he entred in to a shyppe / and his disciples folowed him. And beholde there arose a greate tempest in the see / in so moche that the shippe was covered with waves / and he was a slepe. And his disciples came vn to him / and awoke him sayinge: master save vs / we perishe. And he sayd vnto them: why are ye fearfull / o ye of lytell faithe? Then he arose / and rebuked the wyndes and the see / and their folowed a greate calme. And the men marveyled and sayd: what man is this / that bothe wyndes and see obey hym?[5]
>
> [Matthew, 8, 1534 ed.]

This 'chronicle' style – it could almost be Malory – largely made up of short main statements linked by 'ands', is Tyndale's basic Bible prose. He came to use it the more readily as he began his work of translation with the four Gospels and their essentially chronicle narrative. When he moved from narrative to exhortation (the Sermon on the Mount, the Epistles) and prophecy (Revelation) he could call more rhetoric to his aid. His Pentateuch, which tells the Old Testament story, reverts to the sentence-structure of Alfredian prose.

His choice of chronicle narrative, with paratactic or cumulative main statements, with occasional simple subordination, was reinforced by the Greek of the New Testament (and later by the Hebrew of the Old). For sentences at a time, Tyndale does no more than follow precisely the word-order and syntax of the Greek. Unlike the Wycliffite translators who were wrestling with the periodic Latin of the Vulgate (which will not go into English without a conscious alteration of word-order) he found that he was dealing with tongues equipped with a familiar sentence-structure:

> For the Greek tongue agreeth more with the English than with the Latin. And the properties of the Hebrew tongue agreeth a thousand times more with the English than with the Latin. The manner of speaking is both one; so that in a thousand places thou needest but to translate it into the English word for word; when thou must seek a compass in the Latin, and yet shall have much work to translate it well-favouredly ...[6]
> [*Obedience of a Christian Man*, 1528, 'Preface to the Reader', *mod. sp.*]

Tyndale's stamp on the narrative portions of subsequent versions of the Scriptures was indelible. In the Matthew passage cited above, Coverdale repeated Tyndale word for word, with the one exception of altering 'Master' to 'Lord'. The Great Bible and the Geneva are virtually Tyndale. Rheims takes a more independent line, but some of its key phrases, like 'O ye of little faith', are still inescapably Tyndale's. The Authorised Version makes only a few adjustments:

> And when he was entered into a ship, his disciples followed him. And behold, there arose a great tempest in the Sea, insomuch that the ship was couered with the waues: but he was asleepe. And his disciples came to him, and awoke him, saying, Lord, saue us: we perish. And he saith vnto them, Why are ye fearefull, O ye of little faith? Then he arose, and rebuked the winds and the Sea, and there was a great calme. But the men marueiled, saying, What maner of man is this, that euen the winds and the Sea obey him?

This is still Tyndale, but Tyndale subtly altered. A century of scholarship is no longer satisfied with rendering every Greek connective by 'and'. Two 'buts' replace Tyndale 'ands'; two main statements become sub-ordinated ('*when* he was entered'; 'saying' for 'and sayd'). The Authorised, based on a series of Bibles designed not for private reading but to be read aloud in church, balked at Tyndale's bare translation of the final sentence and inserted four words that added nothing to meaning, altered the mono-syllabic 'bothe' to the disyllabic (and probably more accurate) 'euen', giving the final sentence a new rhythm. Italics mark the new words:

> What *maner of* man is this, that euen *the* winds and *the*
> Sea obey him?

'What maner' had been in the Great Bible. Only the Authorised achieved
the final synthesis of great public spoken prose.

The second layer of biblical prose is exhortation. Here the Greek used
considerable rhetoric: the 'like beginnings', 'like endings', chiasmus, and
parallelisms of Corinthians 13 are in the Greek, and Tyndale had to do no
more than follow his announced principles of translation to produce:

> Love suffreth longe / and is corteous. Love envieth not. Love doth not
> frowardly / swelleth not dealeth not dishonestly / seeketh not her
> awne / is not provoked to anger / thynketh not evyll / reioyseth not in
> iniquite: but reioyseth in the trueth / suffreth all thinge / beleveth all
> thynges / hopeth all thynges / endureth in all thynges.

Throughout the various versions of the sixteenth century we can see the
final version shaping up. Tyndale was no preacher. His skill was in the
sober chronicle style and the great phrase (his is the 'sounding brass' and
the 'tinkling cymbal') rather than in liturgical movement. Coverdale, a
preacher, eased out the movement of a few phrases (his is the 'is not puft
vp' of the final version, and he smoothed out Tyndale's roughness into the
regular rhetoric of 'beareth all thinges, beleueth all thinges, hopeth all
thinges, suffreth all thinges'). Rheims (going back to the Vulgate) read
'charitie' for 'love', and it remained for the 1611 translators to pull it all
together, to adjust Greek rhetoric, Tyndale's great phrases, and the Douai
'charity' to their sense of rhythmical prose for pulpit delivery, to produce
the inevitability of the familiar final version.

Coverdale's sense of what could be effectively read aloud (rather than
what could be meaningfully read in private, which was what Geneva
derived from Tyndale) is best seen in his own sections of the Old Testament, notably in the Prophets and the Psalter:

> Haue mercy vpon me (O God) after thy goodness, and accordinge
> vnto thy greate mercies, do away myne offences.
> Wash me well fro my wickedness, and clense me fro my synne. For
> I knowlege my fautes, and my synne is euer before me.
> [Psalm 50 (51 in A.V.)]

This is quite different from the 'chronicle' prose of Tyndale. The Hebrew
parallelism shapes the syntax but is adapted to English structure. It is pre-
eminently a prose that can be intoned, and Coverdale's Psalter is still that
of the Prayer-book. Coverdale's instinct for native English is as fine as

Tyndale's – but he draws on different sources. The resemblance of the above to the Middle English version done about 1300 is too striking to be accidental:

> Have mercy on me, God, after thy michel mercy; and efter the mychelnes of thy pites do away my wickednes.
>
> Whasshe me more of my wickednes, and clense me of myn synne.
>
> For ich knowe my wickedness, and my synne is evermore ogains me.[7]

Whereas the Authorised Version preserves Tyndale in the narrative sections, in the Hebrew poetry and prophecy of the Bible it sweeps beyond Coverdale. Something of the latinity of Hooker and Cranmer affects the 1611 translators as they work over books like Isaiah or Jeremiah or Revelation, where they allow themselves an expanded rhythm and vocabulary. The Latin polysyllables reverberate: *lamentation, desolation, abomination, testimony, adversary, multitude, innumerable, derision, transgression, iniquity, tribulation.* Extensive illustration is needless: this new expanded rhythm and latinate vocabulary can be readily seen in a comparison between the versions of the 51st Psalm cited and that of the Authorised Version:

> Have mercie upon mee, O God, according to thy loving kindness; according unto the multitude of thy tender mercies blot out my transgressions. Wash mee thoroughly from mine iniquitie, and clense me from my sinne. For I acknowledge my transgressions, and my sinne is ever before me.

The prose of the Authorised Version is thus a prose of considerable range, drawing as occasion demands on both sides of the renaissance conception of the use of English, the native continuity and humanist virtuosity. Structurally, it leans towards Alfredian simplicity. In vocabulary it tends to be archaic, verging on archaic even as Tyndale wrote it and certainly archaic when his language was reprinted in 1611. From the beginning it was a special kind of prose. For all its structural simplicity, and however concrete and homely its illustrations, it was never the language of everyday life. The sacredness of the subject-matter and the setting in which it was heard kept it apart.

Although the structural movement of the biblical sentence is predominantly chronicle, the language of the originals and of all the translations is shot through with metaphor. The imagery of the poetry of a pastoral and oriental people gives it a remoteness and colour that were alien to English chronicle prose. Corn and oil, green pastures, chariots, potsherds, milk and honey, cedars and fig-trees, locusts, the desert and the wilderness, the imagery of richness – the gold and brass and purple and scarlet and fine linen, beryls and jaspers – all of this had illuminated mediaeval English poetry. Now it became part of a sixteenth-century English prose of an essentially new kind: close to speech movement because the ordinary man must understand; consciously rhythmical because it will be heard in a liturgical setting; resonant with the overtones of metaphor that had previously been consistently heard only in poetry.The Bible established prose as a literary vehicle for the serious writer on the most serious and elevated subject.

Before the sixteenth-century debate on the adequacy of English as a prose medium had died down, Tyndale and his successors were creating the first English prose classic. It is this achievement, rather than any impact of its style, which determines its place in the later development of English prose. The familiarity of later writers with the language of the Bible needs no demonstration. Biblical phrases lie embedded in many pages of English prose from the seventeenth century to the present day. But they remain always a thing apart from the movement of the writer's own prose. He knows, and his audience knows, that he is citing Scripture. To both reader and writer the words are so familiar that quotation marks are unnecessary. Those few writers who allow their own *styles* to be strongly moulded by the Scriptures (Carlyle, Ruskin, William Morris, Blake in the *Prophetic Books*, the Butcher and Lang translation of Homer, even Bunyan) are exotics, out of the main current. In the centuries following 1611, English prose will move from triumph to triumph: Donne, Milton, Hobbes, the philosophers, the essayists and the novelists use prose as a great instrument. Stylistically, their debt to the Bible is slight or at most peripheral. In other ways they owe it everything. After 1611 the whole range of human experience from the most trivial to the most sacred was within the ambit of English prose.

Notes

1 The quotations on pp. 95–6 are from A. W. POLLARD, *Records of the English Bible*, London, 1911.
2 POLLARD, *op. cit.*, 307.
3 W. F. MOULTON, *The History of the English Bible*, London, n.d., 70–2.
4 H. WALTER, ed., *Doctrinal Treatises*, Parker Society, Cambridge, 1848, 149, 'Tyndale's Preface to the Obedience of a Christen Man'.
5 This, and other quotations from versions before 1611 from *The English Hexapla*, London, 1841.
6 TYNDALE, *op. cit.*, 148.
7 E. BÜLBRING, ed., *Earliest English Prose Psalter*, EETS, 1891, 60.

Part four The Seventeenth Century

Chapter 10

The Seventeenth Century I: Latin-based Prose

By the opening of the seventeenth century, English prose had emerged as an assured and accepted literary medium. The eloquence from the pulpit, and the alternate simplicity and grandeur of the Bible, the elaborate prose of high humanism, and the colloquial panache of the pamphlet spoke on their differing levels with a new assurance and authority. There was still room for controversy on the use of English, and some of it was heated; but the ground of battle has shifted. Although Bacon translated his major philosophical work into Latin in the 1620's, and Milton as late as the 1650's defended himself and his nation in this still European tongue, there were even in the early years of the century no longer any real misgivings about the language in which to write for a public audience.

But how to write English prose? How, even, to write an English sentence? Writers of the calibre of Bacon and Donne and Milton and the Royal Society scientists propounded very different solutions. How to use words? Ben Jonson and Isaak Walton and Roger L'Estrange and John Locke had firm, and differing, views. Their often meticulous concern with the technique of writing prose arose from no idle preoccupation with 'style'. Throughout a century of intense intellectual and political activity, the writing of prose took on, for the first time, an air of assured professionalism. Good writing mattered, as much to the writer of new (and on the surface slight) literary forms like the essay and the Character, as to the weightier authors of sermon and history and philosophical or scientific treatise. The tensions of the time and its continuous concern for appropriate expression make the seventeenth century the period of the richest and most varied English prose.

The Continuation of Ciceronian Prose

The Latin-based periodic sentence fell early out of favour. By the end of the sixteenth century Cicero was already under attack, and the shorter-winded epigrammatic Silver Latin prose of Tacitus and Seneca was being advocated as a better model. But humanist influence still moulds the prose of two major seventeenth-century writers, Raleigh and Milton. Raleigh, writing in the Tower his *History of the World* (published in 1614) was unaffected by the changing fashion. His occasional eloquence (for example, the familiar finale 'O eloquent, just, and mighty Death') comes as a climax to a regular series of sentences of purely Latin periodic structure:

> Surely that great slaughter of so many thousand Assyrians, in the quarrel of Sardanapalus, together with other calamaties of that long and unfortunate war, which overwhelmed the whole country, not ending but with the ruin and utter destruction of Nineveh, must needs have so weakened the state of Assyria, that it could not in thirty years space be able to invade Palestina, which the ancient kings, reigning in Nineveh, had in all their greatness forborne to attempt.
>
> [Book II, Ch. xxiii, *mod. sp.*][1]

> If Perseus had known it before, that his own son should one day be compelled to earn his living by handywork, in a painful occupation, it is like that he would not, as in a wantonness of sovereignty, have commanded these poor men to be slain which had recovered his treasures out of the sea by their skill in the feat of diving.[2]
>
> [Book V, Ch. vi, *mod. sp.*]

Milton's prose is more complex than Raleigh's. The normal sentence-structure is the Ciceronian period, sustained with considerable virtuosity through interlocked subordinate clauses in some of the longest sentences in English:

> Which makes me wonder much that many of the Gentry, studious men, as I heare should engage themselves to write, and speak publickly in her defence, but that I beleeve their honest and ingenuous natures comming to the Universities to store themselves with good and solid learning, and there unfortunately fed with nothing else, but the scragged and thorny lectures of monkish and miserable sophistry, were sent home again with such a scholastical burre in their throats, as hath stopt and hinderd all true and generous philosophy from entring, crackt their voices for ever with metaphysical gargarisms, and hath made them admire a sort of formal outside men prelatically addicted, whose unchast'nd and unwrought minds never yet initiated or subdu'd under the true lore of religion or moral vertue, which two are the best and greatest points of learning, but either slightly train'd up in a kind of hypocritical and hackny cours of literature to get their

living by, and dazle the ignorant, or els fondly over-studied in uselesse controversies, except those which they use with all the specious and delusive suttlety they are able, to defend their prelatical Sparta, having a Gospel and Church-government set before their eyes, as a fair field wherin they might exercise the greatest vertu's, and the greatest deeds of Christian autority in mean fortunes and little furniture of this world, which even the sage heathen writers and those old *Fabritii*, and *Curii* well knew to be a manner of working, then which nothing could lik'n a mortal man more to God, who delights most to worke from within himself, and not by the heavy luggage of corporeal instrument, they understand it not, & think no such matter, but admire & dote upon worldly riches, & honours, with an easie & intemperat life, to the bane of Christianity: yea they and their Seminaries shame not to professe, to petition and never lin pealing our eares that unlesse we fat them like boores, and cramme them as they list with wealth, with Deaneries, and pluralities, with Baronies and stately preferments, all learning and religion will goe underfoot. 3

[*The Reason of Church Government*, 1641]

This was not merely how Milton wrote. It was for him the proper way in which English prose should be written. In his *Apology ... against Smectymnuus* (1642) he attacked Bishop Hall [the 'English Seneca'] as 'one who makes sentences by the statute, as if all above three inches were confiscate'. Hall's prose is 'hopping short in a series of convulsion fits ... instead of well-siz'd periods he greets us with a quantity of thum-ring posies'.4

Had Milton's own prose been nothing but a series of 'well-sized periods', it is doubtful if even its matter would have kept it alive to the present day. His massive Ciceronian progression is offset by features that make the texture of his prose unique. He has a power of striking phrase after memorable phrase of epigrammatic force, which the 'Senecans' must have envied:

A sad spirit wedded to loneliness.
Give me the liberty to know, to utter, and to argue freely according to conscience, above all liberties.
He who destroys a good Book, kills reason itself.

Furthermore, though he is steeped in the humanist tradition, he commands an unparalleled vocabulary drawn from the language of the Elizabethan pamphlet. Bishops 'swagger to the foretop', they 'meddle' and 'dandle', they 'prog and pander for fees', they emit a 'loud stench'. Usages like 'wassail', 'clipper', 'fadge', 'trencher fury', 'juggle', 'gaudy glistering', 'nuzzle' belong to the world of Nashe and Dekker. His classical learning was matched with a knowledge (unusual in his time) of early English, and time and again he will revive an Anglo-Saxon usage with telling force. Milton's prose (say in the *History of Britain*) can be dreary. But at its best, it is a highly effective amalgam of humanist structural complexity and native effectiveness, the latinised polysyllables skilfully counterpointed against the blunt Anglo-Saxon, with a poet's feeling for imagery, Biblical and other, never far distant.

Milton was the last English writer of consequence to use Ciceronian sentence-structure. It has been claimed that the great age of Ciceronian influence was the following century, which produced the eloquence of Chatham, Pitt and Burke, and the rolling periods of Gibbon.[5] What Gibbon and his contemporaries got from Cicero was sentence-length, not sentence-structure. And this is equally true of seventeenth-century ornate prose. Donne, Browne and Jeremy Taylor, even Bacon on occasion, have a mastery of the long sentence; but the articulation of its parts springs from quite different sources.

Tacitus and Seneca

Bacon in the first book of the *Advancement of Learning* (1605) devotes a section to an attack on the Ciceronian style:

> This grew speedily to an excesse: For men began to hunt more after words, than matter, more after the choisenesse of the Phrase, and the round and cleane composition of the sentence, and the sweet falling of the clauses, and the varying and illustration of their workes with tropes and figures: than after the weight of matter ...[6]

The reaction against Cicero had begun with Erasmus in the early sixteenth century. It was continued by the Frenchman Muret, who lectured on Tacitus at Rome in the 1580's, and by Lipsius (born in what is now Belgium) who edited Tacitus in 1575 and Seneca in 1605. To these northern humanists (shades of Matthew Arnold!) Cicero's elaboration was 'Asian'. The Latin of Tacitus and Seneca (the *genus humile* as opposed to the *genus grande*) became the new ideal. What had begun as a humanist reaction to the writing of Latin rapidly took hold on the vernaculars. Montaigne's essays of 1580 represent a new direction for French prose, and the appearance in 1597 of Bacon's first volume of essays mark not only a new literary genre but the beginnings of what is to become the dominant English prose of the seventeenth century.[7]

Bacon, who began it all, soon reacted against its extremest form, and the later editions of his essays (1612, 1625) were rewritten in a looser style. When he came to issue in 1623 the *De Augmentis Scientiarum*, the 'European' Latin version of his *Advancement of Learning* of 1605, he added a short section, noting that the prose of Seneca, Tacitus, and the younger Pliny with its 'pointed' vocabulary and compressed sentence-structure ('verba ... aculeata, sententiae concisae') had begun to suit the ears of his own age ('atque nostri temporis auribus coepit esse non ita pridem accommodatum').[8] By 1623 he was prepared to include this manner of writing, as well as the Ciceronian, among the 'vanities in studies'.

It was too late to protest. The new manner (which some now called 'Attic') as it was to develop in the seventeenth century did not merely suit the ears of the time. It suited its mode of thought. The Ciceronian period with its unified and architectural planning, its end foreseen in its beginning, implies settled convictions. The exploratory, doubting and increasingly sceptical mind of seventeenth-century England could not think in such linguistic structures. The new prose of short statements, to which fresh ideas could be immediately added by parataxis or simple coordination, allowed a writer like Donne or Burton to think in the act of writing. By the middle of the seventeenth century it was an English prose quite independent of its earlier stage of imitation of Silver Latin.

But this is to leap ahead. The Latin of Seneca, which caught hold of the imagination of the period, was a jerky prose which tended to avoid subordination:

> Enumerare omnes fatorum vias longum est. Hoc unum scio: omnia mortalium opera mortalitate damnata sunt, inter peritura vivimus.[9]

> (To list all the ways of fate is tedious. This one thing I know: all the works of mortals are condemned to mortality; we live among things perishable).

Latin with this structure – here four main statements in paratactic relationship – was to form the classical authority for 'Lipsius his hopping style', the 'Laconic', the 'Senecan amble', or (according to taste) the 'convulsion fits' despised by Milton.

To it was added the brilliant compression of Tacitus, who made the individual word work harder than it had ever done in republican Rome, pinning down his victim in a minimum of words:

> Omnium consensu capax imperii nisi imperasset.[10]

The semantic overload packed into the subjunctive *imperasset*, and the syntactical density of the whole defy adequate translation – 'By the agreement of all, capable of imperial rule, if he had not become emperor' ('Everyone thought him a leader of men – till he got the job'). But if Tacitus could not be readily translated, he could be imitated, and the early seventeenth-century writers vied with each other in combining the short sentence movement of Seneca with the 'pregnant' phrase and 'strong line' of Tacitus.

Bacon's 1597 volume of essays initiated the Senecan movement in English:

> Studies serve for pastimes, for ornaments and for abilities. Their chiefe use for pastime is in privatenes and retiring; for ornamente is in discourse, and for abilitie is in judgement. For expert men can execute, but learned men are fittest to judge or censure.[11]
>
> [*Of Studies*, 1597]

As he wrote his later essays he lengthened the Senecan movement, and frequently led up to a Tacitean 'strong line':

> Be not too sensible, or too remembring, of thy Place, in Conversation, and private Answers to Suitors; but let it rather be said; *When he sits in Place, he is another Man.*[12]
>
> [*Of Great Place*, 1625]

Jonson's *Discoveries*, published in the folio of 1641 but written earlier, is virtually a handbook on the writing of the new prose. Jonson distinguishes carefully between its several varieties, the 'brief', the 'concise', and the 'abrupt', but these precise sub-divisions belong only to the first years of the century, and his more general comments:

> Periods are beautiful when they are not too long ...
> Brevity is attained ... in the composition by omitting conjunctions.

adequately indicate the principles on which he wrote.

From the written essay the style spread rapidly to the spoken sermon where it linked with native speech-rhythms to produce the striking prose of Lancelot Andrewes:

> This should have been done; this, the danger: What was done? This the *factum fuisset*; what the *factum est*? All these were undone, and blowen over; all the undermining disappointed; all this murder, and cruelty, and desolation defeated. The mine is discovered, the snare is broken, and we are delivered. All these, the King, Queene, Prince,

Nobles, Bishops, both Houses alive, all; not a haire of any of their heads perished; not so much as the smell of fire in any of their garments.[13]

[*Sermon of the Gunpowder Plot*, preached at Whitehall, Nov. 5, 1606]

The full development of the first stage of Senecan prose can be clearly seen in the popular essayist Owen Felltham, whose *Resolves*, 'written for the middle sort of people', were first published in 1623. Felltham insists on a 'native decencie' and his views on sentence-structure are explicit:

Long and distended clauses, are both tedious to the ear, and difficult for their retaining. A Sentence well couch'd, takes both the sense and the understanding. I love not those Cart-rope speeches that are longer than the memory of man can fathom.[14]

His own prose moves in short spurts like that of Andrewes:

A kemb'd oration will cost both sweat, and the rubbing of the brain. And kemb'd I wish it, not frizzled nor curl'd. Divinity should not lasciviate. Unwormwooded jests I like well; but they are fitter for the Tavern, than the Majesty of a Temple. Christ taught the People with Authority. Gravity becomes the Pulpit.[15]

[*Of Preaching*, 1623]

After the essay, the literary form which consolidated Senecan prose was the Character. Introduced by Joseph Hall (who was to incur Milton's scorn), it continued in popularity through the pages of Overbury, Earle and Thomas Fuller. The prose of the Character was to show the same kind of development as that of the essay. It began, in Hall's *Characterisms of Virtues and Vices* (1608), with the extremist form of the new prose;

His forehead is rugged and severe; able to discountenance villainy; yet his words are more awful than his brow; and his hand than his words; I know not whether he be more feared or loved; both affections are so sweetly contempered in all hearts; the good fear him lovingly; the middle sort love him fearfully; and only the wicked man fears him slavishly without love.[16]

[*The Good Magistrate*]

This staccatto style was not to last very long. It could carry the short gnomic moralising of the early essays and Characters. It suited a highly individual preacher like Andrewes. But it could clearly, as Milton felt, lead to monotony, and quite early in the seventeenth century it gave way to a more relaxed style of greater capacity and still greater possibilities.

Notes

1   *The Works of Sir Walter Raleigh*, Oxford, 1829, iv, 673.
2   *Ibid.*, vii, 896.
3   *The Works of John Milton*, Columbia edition, New York, 1931, iii, 272–4.
4   *Ibid.*, iii, 321.
5   G. S. GORDON, ed., *English Literature and the Classics*, Oxford, 1912, 142, 'Ciceronianism', by A. C. CLARK.
6   BACON, *The Advancement of Learning*, 1605, 18^r, 18^v.
7   The Senecan influence is the subject of important articles by M. Croll. See the bibliography.
8   J. SPEDDING, and others ed., *The Works of Francis Bacon*, London, 1858, i, 452.
9   SENECA, *Ad Lucilium Epistolae Morales*, Loeb ed., 1920, ii, 438.
10 TACITUS, *Histories*, I, xlix.
11 BACON, *Essays*, World's Classics reprint of 1597 and 1625 editions, 1937, 251.
12 *Ibid.*, 46.
13 LANCELOT ANDREWES, *XCVI Sermons*, quoted from 3rd. ed., 1635, 895.
14 FELLTHAM, *Resolves*, from 8th. imp., 1661, 40.
15 *Ibid.*, 41.
16 R. ALDINGTON, ed., *A Book of 'Characters'*, London, 1924, 65.

Chapter 11

The Seventeenth Century II:
'Loose and free' and the Baroque

The real importance of the Senecan fashion was that it finally provided a century, that still had a respect for Latin models, with classical authority for a sentence-structure and a sentence progression that was unashamedly native. Once it was accepted that good 'classical' English prose need not be Ciceronian but could consist of a series of short main statements set side by side, or, at the most lightly linked by coordinating conjunctions, the way was open for the next phase. Some hint of this is given by Burton, who describes his own style in the preface to the *Anatomy of Melancholy* (1621):

> An extemporean stile ... writ with as small deliberation as I doe ordinarily speak, without all affectation of big words, fustian phrases, jingling termes, tropes, strong lines ...

Burton is not so naively 'extemporean' as he suggests. Earlier in the preface, echoing Bacon, he clearly isolated the styles available for the early seventeenth-century writer:

> He respects matter, thou art wholly for words; he loves a loose and free stile, thou art all for neat composition, strong lines ...

By the later editions of the *Anatomy*, he had increased the list of styles of which he disapproved, adding to the original 'neat composition' and 'strong lines', 'hyperboles' and 'allegories'. His final comprehensive condemnation included thus the Ciceronian period, Tacitean compression, and a whole range of rhetorical decoration.[1]

Burton and Bacon were the most consistent exponents of the 'loose and free' style; it was the basis for the more elaborate prose of Donne, Browne, and Taylor. The terms 'loose' and 'free' can be readily misunderstood, and were generally misunderstood by nineteenth-century grammarians like Bain, who used 'loose' (with its modern overtone of 'slapdash') as a term of condemnation, and so perpetuated an error still embedded in modern grammars.[2] 'Loose' to a seventeenth-century writer meant simply non-Ciceronian and implied a Senecan basis; 'free' described a sentence-structure in which the clauses were not interlocked but each emerged from the previous by a process of accretion. The style, as the following long sentence from *The Advancement of Learning* (1605) indicates, was that of the most serious exposition:

> And so Seneca, after he had consecrated that *Quinquennium Neronis* to the eternall glorie of learned governors, held on his honest and loyall course of good and free counsell, after his maister grew extreamly corrupt in his government; neither can this point otherwise be: for learning endueth mens mindes with a true sence of the frailtie of their persons, the casualtie of their fortunes, and the dignitie of their soule and vocation; so that it is impossible for them to esteeme that any greatnesse of their owne fortune can bee, a true or worthy end of their being and ordainment; and therefore are desirous to give their account to God, and so likewise to their maisters under God (as kinges and the states that they serve) in these words; *Ecce tibi lucrefeci*, and not *Ecce mihi lucrefeci*: whereas, the corrupter sort of meere Politiques, that have not their thoughts established by learning in the love and apprehension of dutie, nor never looke abroad into universalitie; do referre all thinges to themselves, and thrust themselves into the centre of the world, as if all lynes should meet in them and their fortunes; never caring in all the tempests what becomes of the shippe of estates, so they may save themselves in the cockeboat of their owne fortune, whereas men that feele the weight of dutie, and know the limits of selfe-love, use to make good their place and duties, though with peril.[3]
>
>   [*Advancement of Learning*, 1605]

This sentence is Ciceronian in its length, and so is comparable with the long sentence previously cited from Milton. But that is the only point of resemblance. The punctuation in Milton merely indicates where the reader may draw breath; the sentence presses on. In Bacon's sentence, the reader may stop at almost any punctuation point, sometimes even at a comma, and at each such point the sense is complete. Each new clause in Bacon makes an addition or a modification to what has already been said. It is the order of a man thinking as he goes.

The result is the basic prose style of the middle years of the century. Subordination is at a minimum. The sentence proceeds in what is virtually a series of main statements, each developing from the last. These are linked together in one of three ways: parataxis combined with juncture; coordination introduced usually by such words as 'and', 'but', 'nor', 'neither', or 'for'; and a kind of quasi-subordination, where the link-word is usually 'as', 'that', 'where', or 'which'. The punctuation, carefully inserted at

the link points, follows the syntax of its time, not that of the present day.
    Parataxis combined with juncture can be seen in the clauses italicised in
the following:

> We account it a great glory for a man to have his table furnished with
> a variety of meats, but heare the physitian, *hee pulls thee by the eare as*
> *thou sittest*, and telleth thee, that nothing can bee more noxious to
> thine health than such variety and plenty.[4]
>
> [BURTON, *Anatomy of Melancholy*, 1621]

> His daughter finding him indisposed asked whether shee should send
> unto mee, *hee putt it off*, and soone after was found dead.[5]
>
> [BROWNE, *Letters*, 1676]

The coordinated group of clauses is extremely frequent:

> It was his Fathers, and so his; And his, and so ours; *for* we are not joynt
> purchasers of Heaven with the Saints, *but* we are co-heires with Christ
> Jesus.[6]
>
> [DONNE, *Sermon*, April 30, 1626]

This feature is so common (as it is in modern English) that further illustration is unnecessary. But two points should be noted, in which seventeenth-
century usage differs from that of today. 'Nor' today introduces the second
rejected leg of an alternative. In seventeenth-century prose it adds a new
(but negative) statement. 'For' in seventeenth-century usage seldom adds
a reason for a previous statement. Like 'nor', it is often simply a variant of
'and'. Both are preceded by punctuation.
    Much of what appears to be subordination is really coordination by a
link no longer current: 'as', 'that', 'where' and 'which' introduce clauses
which later grammarians insisted on calling adjectival, and so subordinate.
But it is often impossible to find a precise antecedent:

> I conceive there is a traditional Magick, not learned immediately from
> the Devil, but at second hand from his Scholars, who having once the
> secret betrayed, are able, and do emperically practise without his
> advice, they both proceeding upon the principles of Nature; *where*
> actives aptly conjoyned to disposed passives, will under any Master
> produce their effects.[7]
>
> [BROWNE, *Religio Medici*, 1643]

> In his old age he was very bald (*which* claimed a veneration)[8]
>
> [AUBREY, *Brief Lives*]

It cannot be expected that in a childs age should be the vice of a man; *that* were monstrous as if he wore a beard in his cradle.[9]

[TAYLOR, *Sermons*, 1651]

This distinctive feature of seventeenth-century prose was firmly ironed out of the language by the grammarians of the following century.[10]

The Baroque

This early seventeenth-century shift from tight Senecan structures to the opener movement of the 'loose and free' sees once again the written prose of educated Englishmen reverting to the movement of speech. There was in the century a considerable body of effective but less sophisticated prose where speech is the major basis. This speech-based prose is reserved for the following chapter. The 'loose and free' of men well grounded in Latin was the result of a conscious choice of a firmly controlled style for serious communication. Its final development comes with the massive elaboration of the style in Browne, Donne, and Taylor. To these authors I propose to reserve the term 'baroque'. This term has already been suggested by Croll,[11] but he uses it to cover such different authors as Felltham, Bacon, Wotton, Temple, and Browne, equating their 'energy' and 'motion' with the same features in Bernini and El Greco. Energy and motion are unquestionably marks of baroque architecture; but the overwhelming impression conveyed by the baroque in Rome or Würzburg or Kloster Ettal is that of elaborate decoration. Unless this element of decoration is present in a seventeenth-century writer, I do not include him under the term baroque.

The earlier Senecan-based writers avoid ornateness. With the rejection of Ciceronian amplitude went a rejection of decoration. An occasional simile will pass, but generally Burton's rejection of fustian phrases and tropes and Bacon's description of his *Advancement* as written 'without varnish or amplification' establish the norm. Browne, Donne, and Taylor have no such inhibitions. Accepting without question the accretive sentence-structure of the 'loose and free' style, they add simile, metaphor and a range of daring imagery; they reintroduce many of the tropes and figures of renaissance rhetoric. They are, of course, each different. Each writes in a manner individual and immediately recognisable; but they are alike in all three being acutely aware of the movement of speech on public occasions, Donne and Taylor as preachers, and Browne with his ear for expanded rhythms. To speech movement and the structure of the 'loose

and free' sentence they add their characteristic decorations to produce a
massive ornateness, for which the term baroque is appropriate:

> But the iniquity of oblivion blindely scattereth her Poppy, and deals
> with the memory of Men without distinction to merit of perpetuity.
> Who can but pity the Founder of the Pyramids? Herostratus lives
> that burnt the Temple of Diana, he is almost lost that built it; Time
> hath spared the Epitaph of Adrians Horse, confounded that of him-
> self.[12]

[BROWNE, *Hydriotaphia*, 1658]

Here the structure of the individual clauses and the *but/and/*juncture
links between them are the same as Bacon's. The difference is in the
imagery, the word-rhythm of strategically placed latinised words, and the
elaborate overall rhythm of the paragraph from which this is taken.

Taylor's characteristic decoration by means of extended similes was
much admired in his own day and much derided immediately afterwards.
These very beautiful passages are by way of being set showpieces:

> So have I seen the eye of the world looking upon a fenny bottome,
> and drinking up too free draughts of moysture gather'd them into a
> cloud, and that cloud crept about his face, and made him first look
> red, and then cover'd him with darknesse and artificiall night: so is
> our reason at a feast ...[13]

[*Sermons*, 1653]

Taylor's extended similes include the lark rising, the rose, the fair taper,
the busy flame, the Lybian lion, the humble vine. They emerge from his
prose with all the twining splendour of baroque decor; but the clausal
structure is that of simple cumulation.

Donne in his sermons combines speech movement, the 'loose and free'
structure, and a matchless command of metaphor. His views on prose are
as specific as those of Bacon or Jonson.

> The Holy Ghost in penning the Scriptures delights himself, not only
> with a propriety, but with a delicacy, and harmony, and melody of
> language; with height of Metaphors, and other figures, which may
> work greater impressions upon the Readers, and not with barbarous,
> or triviall, or market, or homely language ... and they mistake it
> much, that thinke, that the Holy Ghost hath rather chosen a low, and
> barbarous, and homely style, then an eloquent, and powerfull manner
> of expressing himselfe.[14]

[*LXXX Sermons*, 1640]

This is a plea for eloquence, but it is not directed towards a return to the Ciceronian sentence. As his own practice shows, he accepted the 'loose and free' sentence-structure of his time. What Donne objected to was the bareness and lack of decoration of the earlier practitioners, and he manipulates cumulative structure, speech movement, and baroque decoration with a new and conscious mastery:

> It comes equally to us all, and makes us all equall when it comes. The ashes of an Oak in the Chimney, are no Epitaph of that Oak, to tell me how high or how large that was; it tels me not what flocks it sheltered while it stood, nor what men it hurt when it fell. The dust of great persons graves is speechlesse too, it sayes nothing, it distinguishes nothing: As soon the dust of a wretch whom thou wouldest not, as of a Prince whom thou couldest not look upon, will trouble thine eyes, if the winde blow it thither; and when a whirle-winde hath blowne the dust of the Church-yard into the Church, and the man sweeps out the dust of the Church into the Church-yard, who will undertake to sift those dusts again, and to pronounce. This is the Patrician, this is the noble flowre, and this the yeomanly, this the Plebeian bran. So is the death of *Jesabel* (*Jesabel* was a Queen) expressed; They shall not say, this is Jesabel; not only not wonder that it is, nor pity that it should be, but they shall not say, they shall not know. This is Jesabel.[15]
>
> [*LXXX Sermons*, 1640]

Senecan prose, which began as a staccato series of short sentences, thus culminates in a new kind of rhetoric. The short sentences remain, but no longer as isolated units. They are subsumed into a massive new unit of paragraph dimensions. Editions with 'modern' punctuation tend to break up these mass movements into several sentences of medium length. The original punctuation (it is used in this chapter) is essential. It preserves both the individuality of the short components and the cumulative flow of the longer unit.

Although the baroque produced some of our greatest prose, the current of fashion was within a few years to run in another direction. Baroque prose remains a glory of the past, not always properly understood even by its defenders: Pearsall Smith, editing Taylor, can write: 'What has English grammar to say about writing which so outrageously flouts its rules?'[16] One might answer (in the words of Strafford defending himself in 1641) 'My Lords, do we not live under the laws? and must we be punished by laws before they are made?' The baroque sentence, like the 'loose and free' from which it evolved, had its own laws, both of punctuation and of syntax. Modern English prose begins from a later date, and its 'rules' were established by eighteenth-century grammarians.

Notes

1 R. BURTON, *Anatomy of Melancholy*, from 3rd. ed., 1628, 10–12.
2 A. BAIN, *English Composition and Rhetoric*, 4th. ed., London, 1893, 91–3. Bain even uses the terms 'viciously loose' p. 93.
3 BACON, *The Advancement of Learning*, 1605, 14 v.
4 R. BURTON, *Anatomy of Melancholy*, part 2, section 2, mem. 1, sub-sect. 2.
5 G. KEYNES, ed., *The Workes of Sir Thomas Browne*, London, 1931, vi, 67, the 'Letters'.
6 JOHN DONNE, *LXXX Sermons*, 1640, 747 (Sermon LXXIII).
7 G. KEYNES, ed., *The Workes of Sir Thomas Browne*, i, 39, *Religio Medici*.
8 A. CLARK, ed., *Brief Lives by John Aubrey*, Oxford, 1898, i, 347.
9 L. P. SMITH, *The Golden Grove. Selected from ... Jeremy Taylor*, Oxford, 1930, 113.
10 H. BLAIR, *Lectures on Rhetoric and Belles Lettres*, 1823 ed., 1, 246–8.
11 MALONE & RUUD (see bibliography), M. CROLL, 'The Baroque Style in English Prose'.
12 *The Workes of Sir Thomas Browne*, op. cit., iv, 46.
13 *The Golden Grove*, op. cit., 152–3.
14 J. DONNE, *LXXX Sermons*, 1640, 556–7 (Sermon LV).
15 *Ibid.*, 148 (Sermon XV).
16 *The Golden Grove*, op. cit., Intro., xl.

Chapter 12

The Seventeenth Century III:
Speech-based Prose

It requires little exploration in the prose of the seventeenth century to find considerable areas of quite plain prose, free from rhetorical devices and from latinised vocabulary, based on a sentence-structure which is loosely jointed but which is manifestly different from the 'loose and free' that evolved from Senecan imitation. Much of it is sub-literary, diaries, private letters and memoirs, accounts of travel, popular journalism, manuals of instruction and the like. Were it all at this sub-literary level, it might be written off as of little account. But prose of this type continually exceeds expectation (often even the expectation of the original author) and forces itself to critical attention: from the diarists emerge Evelyn and Pepys; from the letter-writers emerges Dorothy Osborne; from the notebooks of personal jottings emerge Aubrey's *Brief Lives* and Selden's *Table Talk*; from the memoirs emerges the *Life of Colonel Hutchinson*; from the manuals of instruction *The Compleat Angler*: some of them not written for publication; all of them based on the movement of speech and – in contrast to the prose of the preceding two chapters – not on any consciously formulated theory of prose style.

It was nothing new for speech-based prose to produce writing of literary excellence. Earlier examples have already been discussed. What is new in the seventeenth century is the persistent pressure of speech-based prose on prose of more obvious literary pretentions. It had already transformed the Senecan staccato into a prose of discourse. Now, within a few years of the death of Donne, the baroque sermon was in turn under attack not merely by implication from a non-conformist like Baxter but by direct and reasoned criticism from an Anglican, John Wilkins. Within a few years of the publication of the *altitudo* of *Religio Medici*, Hobbes' *Leviathan* rejected Browne's attitudes and his prose. The middle years of the seventeenth century took a cold look at what passed for scientific writing and moved quietly on to the empiricism of the Royal Society expressed deliberately in the 'language of Artizans, Countrymen, and Merchants'.

This use of speech-based prose can range from the unconscious artistry

of John Bunyan or Dorothy Osborne at one end of the scale to a deliberate
and enunciated choice at the other by Dryden or Boyle. Before the end of
the century it was the only accepted way of writing. Speech-based prose
in the single sentence often differs little if at all from the single sentence of
the 'loose and free'. Read in longer passages, however, there is no question
of its separate identity. The reality, or at least the illusion, of the speaking
voice is transcribed. The following passages, from a letter-writer, a manual-
writer, and a journalist, make no attempt to disguise their ultimate source
in the movement of speech:

> God forgive mee I was as neer Laughing Yesterday where I should
> not; would you beleeve that I had the grace to goe heare a sermon
> upon a week day, in Earnest tis true, and Mr. Marshall was the Man
> that preached, but never any body was soe defeated, hee is soe famed
> that I Expected rare things from him and seriously I listned to him at
> first with as much reverence and attention as if hee had bin St. Paul
> and what doe you think he told us?[1]
>
> [DOROTHY OSBORNE, *Letters to Sir William Temple*, written 1653]

> First, let your Rod be light, and very gentle, I take the best to be of
> two pieces, and let not your line exceed (especially for three or four
> links next to the hook) I say, not to exceed three or four hairs at the
> most, though you may Fish a little stronger above in the upper part
> of your Line: but if you attain to Angle with one hair, you shall have
> more rises and catch more fish.[2]
>
> [WALTON, *The Compleat Angler*, 1653]

> Most certain, 'tis; without that mark men go they know not whether.
> *First*, the *End*; *then*; the *Way*; is (I suppose) the Common Method of
> all Wise Men: and his advice to such, to look before them, might have
> been spared, they would have don't without it. Now to his Businesse;
> but first, I'le clear the way to't. The Question is ...[3]
>
> [R. L'ESTRANGE, *Interest Mistaken, or The Holy Cheat*, 1661]

Three features distinguish prose of this type. The vocabulary is quite
ordinary; there is no straining after effects with unusual words or expressions. Secondly, no grammar yet written offers an adequate description
of its syntactical structuring – indeed the idea of a 'sentence' or of 'sentence-
structure' receives a severe shock when faced with L'Estrange's 'Now to
his Business;' and one would be hard put to explain in traditional terms
the syntax of Walton's 'not to exceed'. We are clearly face to face with
the so far undescribed 'grammar' of spoken English, which is only now

beginning to engage the attention of linguistic scholars. The third feature is astonishing, in the light of the first two: the three passages cited are extremely effective pieces of *written* prose. Not a word could be eliminated or displaced without affecting the meaning or the tone. Their clarity, and non-ambiguity, is absolute. In L'Estrange even the punctuation carries authority, a series of expression-marks indicating the stress, juncture, and intonation of live speech.

Prose of this type, or based on this type, is extremely common in the seventeenth century. It is seen at its least sophisticated level in correspondence, of which the Verney letters are a fair sample. More sophisticated, because they were written for publication, but preserving the conventions of the letter-form and the movement of speech, are James Howell's *Epistolae Ho-Elianae* (1645):

> I pray you leave the smutty Ayr of London, and com hither to breath sweeter, wher you may pluck a Rose, and drink a Cillibub.[4]
>
> [*Letter from Kent*, dated 1625]

It is understandably common in pamphleteering and popular journalism, particularly, as C. V. Wedgwood has noted,[5] during the period of some years in the 1640's when censorship was lifted. During the Civil War a brisk and forthright prose close to common speech was the only medium likely to win the popular ear. From the mass of generally anonymous journalism of the period, two names might be singled out, Sir John Birkenhead who campaigned for the King from Oxford in the *Mercurius Aulicus* (1642-5), and Roger L'Estrange, another King's man, whose numerous pamphlets continued to pour out till almost the end of the century.

With this political journalism is associated in tone and language, if not in theme, the hundreds of publications recounting adventures at home and abroad that formed the reading matter of a large part of the population. Richard Peeke (who fought with a quarterstaff against three Spaniards armed with rapiers and poniards and lived to write it all down) must speak for the whole group:

> I know not what the Court of a King means, nor what the fine phrases of silken Courtiers are. A good ship I know, and a poor cabin; and tha language of a cannon; and therefore as my breeding has been rough, scorning delicacy; and my present being consisteth altogether upon the soldier (blunt, plain, and unpolished) so must my writings be, proceeding from fingers fitter for the pike than the pen.[6]
>
> [R. PEEKE, *Three to One*, 1626, *mod. sp.*]

Since the movement of speech was steadily pressing on the prose of literature, and was, indeed, to reshape it before the century was out, the
question arises (it was debated at least until the early eighteenth century),
whose speech? The language of the Court? The language of polite
society? The Royal Society's choice of the 'language of Artizans, Countrymen, and Merchants'? Setting aside the special case of dramatic writing,
one can distinguish different attitudes. The educated renaissance writer had
been brought up to accept (to requote Greene) 'τὸ πρέπον, a certaine
decorum': the manner should suit the matter. If this lesson was lost on a
pamphleteer like Milton, it was not forgotten by the political journalists
of this time. When L'Estrange wrote for popular consumption, his
language and movement were appropriately colloquial:

> His third query is a frank proposal, without any more ado, of taking
> all Church lands into the Crown: and very courteously he offers all
> poor Cavaliers a Snip in the Booty.[7]
>
> [*A Caveat to the Cavaliers*, 1661]

Yet L'Estrange could write otherwise; when he fell from favour in his
later years he turned to translating the classics in more formal terms.

For the less well educated authors (and this must perforce include the
women of the time) the speech of their sex and class provided the only
basis for written prose. Aphra Behn writes breathless sequences that recall
both Dorothy Osborne's letters and Joyce's Molly Bloom:

> I ought to tell you, that the Christians never buy any slaves but they
> give 'em some name of their own, their native ones being likely very
> barbarous, and hard to pronounce; so that Mr. Trefry gave Oroonoko
> that of Caesar; which name will live in that country as long as that
> (scarce more) glorious one of the great Roman: for 'tis most evident
> he wanted no part of the personal courage of that Caesar, and acted
> things as memorable, had they been done in some part of the world
> replenished with people and historians, that might have given him his
> due. But his misfortune was, to fall in an obscure world, that afforded
> only a female pen to celebrate his fame; though I doubt not but it had
> lived from others endeavours, if the Dutch, who immediately after his
> time took that country, had not killed, banished and dispersed all
> those that were capable of giving the world this great man's life, much
> better than I have done.[8]
>
> [*Oroonoko*, 1688]

Bunyan, with no reading apart from the Bible and his puritan books, had
only two sources to draw on, Scripture and common speech. His Biblical

language and imagery need no illustration. It is what most readers carry away from Bunyan. There is less of it than is commonly imagined. The great bulk of Bunyan's prose is narrative, in the language and movement of the speech of his class, a very high proportion of all his work being in dialogue form. Christian and his companions, Christiana and her family, Mr. Badman, and the Diabolonians on trial faithfully echo the speech habits of Bunyan's level of society:

> At a Summer Assizes holden in Hartford, while the Judge was sitting upon the Bench, comes this old Tod into the Court, cloathed in a green suit, with his Leathern Girdle in his hand, his Bosom open, and all on a dung sweat, as if he had run for his Life ...[9]
>
> [*The Life and Death of Mr. Badman*, 1680]

> Then said Mr. False-Peace, Gentlemen, and you now appointed to be my Judges, I acknowledg that my name is Mr. Peace, but that my name is Mr. False-Peace, I utterly deny. If your Honours shall please to send for any that do intimately know me, or for the midwife that laid my mother of me, or for the Gossips that was at my Christening, they will any or all of them prove that my name is not False-Peace, but Peace.[10]
>
> [*The Holy War*, 1682]

As one moves up the ladder of seventeenth-century society, speech remains the basis for much prose of a quite classic excellence. Walton ('of the City of London, Ironmonger') with no more than a school education, Dryden (Westminster and Trinity College, Cambridge), and Edward Hyde (Magdalen Hall, Oxford, and Middle Temple) who is to become the first Earl of Clarendon, all write an easy, natural prose that has evolved from their conversation with their peers:

> In another walk to Salisbury, he saw a poor man, with a poorer horse, that was fall'n under his load; they were both in distress, and needed present help; which Mr. Herbert perceiving, put off his canonical coat, and help'd the poor man to unload, and after, to load his horse.[11]
>
> [WALTON, *Life of Mr. George Herbert*, 1670]

> To begin, then, with Shakespeare. He was the man who of all modern, and perhaps ancient poets, had the largest and most comprehensive soul. All the images of nature were still present to him, and he drew them, not laboriously, but luckily; when he describes anything, you more than see it, you feel it too.[12]
>
> [DRYDEN, *An Essay of Dramatic Poesy*, 1668]

It was so very late every day before the House was resumed, (the Speaker commonly leaving the chair about nine of the clock, and never resuming it till four in the afternoon) that it was very thin; they only who prosecuted the bill with impatience remaining in the House, and the others who abhorred it, growing weary of so tiresome an attendance, left the House at dinner-time, and afterwards followed their pleasures: so that my Lord Falkland was wont to say that they who hated bishops hated them worse than the devil, and they who loved them did not love them so well as their dinner.[13]

[CLARENDON, *History of the Rebellion*, iii, 241, written 1646–8]

Prose of this type is not based on just any speech; it is based on the speech of quiet and unemphatic conversation, with an insistent bias towards plainness. Some of it may be the result of unconscious choice; in two kinds of writing, the sermon and the prose of science, the choice becomes more deliberate as the century proceeds. The downright Latimer-Jewell-Smith reformation sermon of the sixteenth century had yielded to the varying elaborations of Andrewes, Donne, and Taylor, preaching at Whitehall, Paul's Cross, or elsewhere to admiring and quiescent congregations who were interested in effective imagery and rhetoric rather than in religious controversy. But controversy and tension became once again the pattern, in the mid-years of the century. The battle for men's minds was on again, and it had to be won in the speech of common men.

In any event, eloquence was instinctively felt to be out of place in the country parishes. George Herbert, who died before the mid-century storm, preached (as he well could, having been Public Orator at Cambridge) one 'florid' sermon to his parishioners at Bemerton, and then announced:

That should not be his constant way of preaching ... for their sakes, his language and his expressions should be more plain and practical in his future sermons.[14]

[WALTON, *Life of Herbert*]

After his death there was published in 1640 his *Jacula Prudentum*, a volume of homely proverbs he had collected to reinforce the colloquial sermons he had promised. Many Anglican preachers, while they disagreed with the doctrinal stand of the parliamentary chaplain Richard Baxter, could agree with his views on preaching:

Indeed, the more I have to do with the ignorant sort of people the more I find that we cannot possibly speak too plainly to them. If

we do not speak to them in their own vulgar dialect, they understand us not.[15]

[*Reliquiae Baxterianae*, pub. 1696]

It fell to a future bishop to formulate these attitudes into a coherent theory
of sermon-prose: John Wilkins' *Ecclesiastes, or a discourse concerning the Gift
of Preaching, as it falls under the Rules of Art* (1646) condemned the baroque
and the rhetorical and set up the virtues of colloquial plainness in their
stead. Wilkins was extremely influential, whether as preacher, master of a
college, convener of weekly discussions on 'experimental philosophy' and
later as a secretary of the Royal Society. His views on the prose of the
sermon set the tone for the Restoration preaching of men like Tillotson
and Stillingfleet, and they found ample support in the tastes of the returned
Charles:

> The King had little or no literature, but true and good sense: and he
> had got a right notion of style: for he was in *France* at a time when
> they were much set on reforming their language ... So this help'd to
> raise the value of these men, when the King approv'd of the style their
> discourses generally ran in; which was clear, plain, and short.[16]

[G. BURNET, *History of My Own Times*, written 1683ff.]

The King's tastes and the influence of the seventeenth-century French
deals of prose would have had little effect if the movement towards speech-
based prose had not been already firmly established. Robert South speaks
not only for his brother preachers in the 1660's but for a whole generation
of predecessors:

> A second property of the ability of speech, conferred by Christ upon
> his apostles, was its unaffected plainness and simplicity; it was to be
> easy, obvious and familiar; with nothing in it strained or far-fetched;
> no affected scheme, or airy fancies, above the reach or relish of an
> ordinary apprehension ... For there is a certain majesty in plainness;
> as the proclamation of a prince never frisks it in tropes or fine con-
> ceits, in numerous and well-turned periods, but commands in sober,
> natural expressions ... In a word, the apostles' preaching was therefore
> mighty and successful, because plain, natural and familiar, and by no
> means above the capacity of their hearers; nothing being more pre-
> posterous than for those who were professedly aiming at men's
> hearts, to miss the mark by shooting over their heads.[17]

[*Sermon preached on the 30th of April, 1668*]

The year before this sermon was preached there appeared another well-
known prescription for effective written prose:

They have therefore been most rigorous in putting in execution the only Remedy, that can be found for this *extravagance*: and that has been, a constant Resolution, to reject all the amplifications, digressions, and swellings of style: to return back to the primitive purity, and shortness, when men deliver'd so many *things*, almost in an equal number of *words*. They have exacted from all their members, a close, naked, natural way of speaking; positive expressions; clear senses; a native easiness; bringing all things as near the Mathematical plainness, as they can: and preferring the language of Artizans, Countrymen, and Merchants, before that, of Wits, or Scholars.[18]

[THOS. SPRAT, *History of the Royal Society*, 1667]

The Royal Society, founded in 1660 'for the Improvement of Natural Knowledge', gathered together in its early years a remarkable group, bishops and dons, poets, noblemen, and private gentlemen, who met weekly to see an experiment conducted or hear a scientific report. Their insistence on the inductive method, expressed in plain prose, had its roots earlier in the century. Bacon, writing 'without varnish'[19] his *Advancement*, was in one sense their founder. John Wilkins, the advocate of plain preaching in 1646, presided both in London and in Oxford in the Commonwealth days over an 'invisible college' (the phrase is Boyle's) which discussed natural philosophy. He was on friendly terms with the Cambridge platonists at Emmanuel, from which emerged Cudworth's plain and unaffected writing. Working independently, Hobbes published in 1651 his scientific analysis of the State, *Leviathan*. His chapter 'Of Speech' makes it evident that for Hobbes there was no sharp dividing line between written and spoken expression. Like all the writers of this group he is for plain diction: among his 'causes of absurdity' in reasoning is 'the use of Metaphors, Tropes, and other Rhetoricall figures'.[20]

What the establishment of the Royal Society did was to give final printed authority, under distinguished patronage, for an English prose which rejected all Latin syntax (both Ciceronian and Senecan), rejected renaissance rhetorical figures, rejected metaphor and simile, and reverted to essentially Anglo-Saxon sentence-structure. Joseph Glanvill, writing some years before he became a member of the Society, and Boyle, writing after he became a foundation member, write the same kind of neutral, speech-based prose:

It seems impossible that a wheel should move ... For let's suppose the wheel to be divided according to the Alphabet. Now in motion there is a change of place, and in the motion of a wheel there is a succession of one part to another in the same place; so that it seems inconceivable that A should move until B hath left its place: For A cannot move, but it must acquire some place or other. It can acquire none but what was B's, which we suppose to be most immediate to it. The same place cannot contain them both. And therefore B must leave its place, before A can have it: Yea, and the nature of succession requires it. But now B cannot move, but into the place of C ...[21]

[JOSEPH GLANVILL, *The Vanity of Dogmatising*, 1661]

We took a new pewter-bottle, capable to contain, as we guessed, about half a pint of water, and having filled it top full with that liquor, we screwed on the stopple, and exposed it during a very frosty night to the cold air, and the next morning the water appeared to have burst the bottle, though its matter was metalline; and though purposely for this trial we had chosen it quite new, the crack appeared in the very substance of the pewter. This experiment we repeated.[22]

[R. BOYLE, *New Experiments and Observations touching Cold*, 1665]

This is certainly a 'close, naked, natural way of speaking'. But, in spite of Sprat, it is difficult to hear it as the language of Artizans, Countrymen, and Merchants, whose actual speech was captured by Bunyan rather than by the savants. Royal Society prose was an artifact, derived from the speech of polite society, as much a piece of experimental apparatus as the numerous 'Instruments' so admiringly catalogued by Sprat. It was a major discovery in communication. Its influence was to dominate the next hundred years. And it is still felt.

The hundred years before 1660 remains one of the great periods of English prose. With Nashe, Hooker, the Bible, Donne, and Milton at one pole and Bacon, Walton, and the Royal Society at the other, English prose has never shown such diversity and such capability. It could be a musical instrument, superbly played; it could be a scientific instrument, delicately adjusted. In the next hundred years there are to be further, and massive, gains. There are also to be considerable losses. The sermon never recovered. The glories of baroque prose could not be revived. The pamphlet wilted as the language of polite society became the norm. The masterful discursiveness of *Urn-Burial* and *The Anatomy of Melancholy* was disciplined out of the language. But the essay and the novel were in the near future, and the losses must be balanced against the gains.

What finally emerged in the 1660's as the basis of the new written prose was the speech of the upper reaches of English society. True, only a minority of the writers of the time belonged there by birth. But entry for the young man of tolerable background with the requisite ability was not impossibly difficult; learning was allowable, if it were carried lightly, and expressed with 'ease'. The renaissance individualistic display of personal virtuosity, the ambitious parade of rhetoric and learning, no longer dazzled. The scholar has been displaced by the gentleman. So Cowley, Congreve, and Dryden, who capture the required tone of apparently effortless easiness, not Bacon, Burton, and Browne, were to form the starting-point for the next development.

Notes

1   G. C. MOORE SMITH, ed., *The Letters of Dorothy Osborne to Sir William Temple*, Oxford, 1928, 85.
2   I. WALTON, *The Compleat Angler*, Ch. V.
3   R. L'ESTRANGE, *Interest Mistaken, or The Holy Cheat*, 1661, 124.
4   JAMES HOWELL, *Epistolae Ho-Elianae*, 1625 entry, from 2nd ed., 1650, 105.
5   C. V. WEDGWOOD, *Poetry and Politics under the Stuarts*, Cambridge, 1962, 71–2.
6   C. H. FIRTH, ed., *Stuart Tracts 1603–1693*, London, 1903, 274–93.
7   R. L'ESTRANGE, *A Caveat to the Cavaliers*, 1661, 23.
8   APHRA BEHN, *Shorter Novels*, Everyman edition, 1930, 186, 'Oroonoko'.
9   J. BROWN, ed., *Bunyan's The Life and Death of Mr. Badman*, Cambridge, 1905, 27.
10 J. BROWN, ed., *Bunyan's The Holy War*, Cambridge, 1905, 307.
11 G. SAINTSBURY, ed., *Walton's Lives*, World's Classics reprint, 305.
12 W. P. KER, ed., *The Essays of John Dryden*, Oxford, 1900, i, 79.
13 W. D. MACRAY, ed., *Clarendon's History of the Rebellion*, Oxford, 1888, i, 363.
14 SAINTSBURY, *op. cit.*, 295.
15 F. J. POWICKE, *The Life of the Revd. Richard Baxter*, London, 1924, 282–3.
16 O. AIRY, ed., *G. Burnet's History of My Own Time*, Oxford, 1897, i, 340.
17 H. J. C. GRIERSON, *Rhetoric and English Composition*, Edinburgh, 1945, 44–6.
18 THOMAS SPRAT, *History of the Royal Society*, 1667, 113, (facsimile reprint 1959).
19 BACON, *The Advancement of Learning*, 1605, 27^r.
20 A. R. WALLER, ed., *Hobbes' Leviathan*, Cambridge, 1904, 25.
21 JOSEPH GLANVILL, *The Vanity of Dogmatising*, 1661, 55.
22 ROBERT BOYLE, *New Experiments and Observations touching Cold*, 1665, 297.

Part five The Creation of Modern Prose

Chapter 13

The Century of Prose 1660-1760

One of the commonest descriptions of the eighteenth century is the 'Age of Prose'. It is a concept that calls for close examination. If prose means the whole range of the medium, then the century of *Areopagitica* and *Leviathan* has an equal claim to the title. If prose here means (as indeed it inevitably does) the medium of which Addison and Swift are the great exemplars, the concept of a uniform 'period' of prose extending from 1700 to 1800 is an illusion. The prose of *Gulliver*, the *Spectator*, *Pamela*, and *The Citizen of the World* belongs to the same register. The prose of *Tristram Shandy*, *The Decline and Fall of the Roman Empire*, *The Man of Feeling*, and *Fingal* belongs to quite another. Only exceptionally will an eighteenth-century author move between the two, and the effect is (and was) disconcerting. From the sole evidence of the prose of Horace Walpole's letters, it would be difficult to assign to him the authorship of *The Castle of Otranto*. His original readers (similarly misled) 'believed it to be Mr. Gray's'.[1]

Yet the idea of an age of prose about this general period of time is too deeply embedded in English literary history to be lightly abandoned. The sensitive reader rightly insists on its reality. The problem is to establish its proper limits so that the concept agrees with the facts. If one isolates the elements that make up the central prose of the Augustan period in the early years of the eighteenth century, and looks forwards and backwards in time from that viewpoint, a unified period of prose does emerge. It is the hundred years between 1660 and 1760. Accepting Swift and Addison as criteria, one is conscious between these two dates (as never before or afterwards) of a remarkable measure of agreement between writer and reader – whatever their social class – of what constituted an acceptable way of writing. The speech-based prose that finally triumphed in the third quarter of the seventeenth century remained dominant for these hundred years.

The upper and lower limits of this century of prose can be set with some precision. Before 1660 elaborate and baroque prose was still possible; after that date only ease and plainness guaranteed a hearing. At the lower end of the hundred years, it remained possible to write prose of colloquial ease – Goldsmith's *Citizen of the World*, one of the high points of eighteenth-century familiar prose, appeared in 1760–1. But something has happened. Between 1660 and 1760, it is no exaggeration to say, one can read dozens of books by men and women, ranging from the fully professional to the writer of private memoranda, without coming across a single page that deviates from the essentially colloquial norm of the time. It is difficult in this period to find *any* bad prose. After 1760 bad prose is only too easy to find. There is also, after 1760, good prose of a kind that owes little if anything to the norms of Addison and Swift. Gibbon and Burke represent a fresh start. The Augustan criteria no longer necessarily apply. The old agreement between reader and writer has broken down.

The taste of the general reading public between 1660 and 1760 was, on the face of it, of a very high order. It made best-sellers of *An Essay on Dramatic Poesy*, *Gulliver's Travels*, the *Spectator*, *Robinson Crusoe* and *Pamela*. These were all written within the terms of the tacit 'agreement', a prose style close to the movement of speech, and (as even Defoe was prepared to advocate) the speech of gentlemen at that. After 1760 public taste appears to change, ready to welcome what was almost a new kind of baroque prose; and with the change in taste came a loss of the previous apparently effortless discrimination. Thomas Gray and the Fellows at Pembroke were impressed by *The Castle of Otranto* (1764) and made no objection to the excited and fustian prose in which it was written.[2] At the beginning of this decade there was equal enthusiasm, among both unsophisticated and learned alike, for the new emotional overtones and sinuous sentence-structure of *Tristram Shandy* (1759–67) and the bombastic and rhythmical rant of Macpherson's Ossianic translations (1760–3). Within the same few years there were the first complaints by academic grammarians that Swift's style was too lax. Such a confluence of popular taste and academic opinion is a clear indication that a well-defined period of prose had come to an end.

It would be easy to see in this loss of discrimination the results of the widening of the reading public that is a feature of the time. This explanation can be no more than partial. Ian Watt has demonstrated that the widening of the reading public though real was not spectacular; there was no mass dilution.[3] Besides, intelligent and well-educated men were enraptured in the 1760's by prose which today is accounted negligible: witness Gray and *Otranto*, and the rigorous Hugh Blair, who quite genuinely thought Ossian 'sublime'. The explanation must be sought elsewhere.

In spite of its apparent infallibility in picking winners, I think one tends to over-estimate the literary sensitivity of the reading public between 1660 and 1760. Once speech-based prose became the established norm, it was both good sense and good fashion for a writer to be simple and clear. Swift commended the practice of Lord Falkland[4] who read his manuscript to a chamber maid and eliminated what she could not understand. He followed the same practice himself.[5] The writer in the age of prose adjusted his style to a wide range of readers. The wide variety of readers, on their side, faced with speech-based prose, were in possession of an automatically built-in standard of judgement, which came not from wide literary reading but from instinctive listening. So long as what they read did not deviate from the movement of natural speech, and particularly the speech of their betters, it was acceptable. They were led to expect colloquial sentence-structure with its loose accretion of clauses; direct and simple vocabulary in close contact with everyday life; a total absence of exotic imagery, intrusive rhetoric, or 'poetic' rhythms. The age of prose represents a triumph of agreed convention. The skill and taste were all on the writer's side. In the 1760's, once something other than polite conversation became a possible norm, the reader's built-in responses no longer provided any sure guidance. New criteria had to be painfully created. It was to be some time before the sensitive skill of Sterne overtook the mechanical rumble of Macpherson in general critical esteem.

The principles of the prose-writing in this age are made explicit in two writers of central importance, Swift and Defoe. Together they represent the two classes who are to be mainly responsible for the creation of the prose of the period. Swift belongs to the more privileged group. Religion and ability gave him access to university, a classical training in Latin and Greek, familiarity for a few formative years with the upper reaches of English society, and a life-long friendship with similarly educated men of letters of his day. For the son of a dissenter and tallow-chandler, like Defoe, the way up was more difficult. But it was at least easier than Bunyan's private struggle towards literacy a generation earlier. After the Act of Uniformity of 1662, dissenters were excluded from Oxford and Cambridge, and dissenting schoolmasters were barred from teaching in the ordinary schools. The Act of Toleration of 1689 made teaching in other institutions possible, and the dissenters set up a series of 'academies'.[6] Defoe attended the academy at Stoke Newington, studying the characteristic blend of English, mathematics, and modern languages that was to become the mark of the dissenting educational tradition.

Such disparity in background should have produced very divergent attitudes to the writing of prose, and of course the prose style of each is unmistakably distinctive. But the divergencies are less striking than the similarities. They are both men of their age. Swift inherited the Restoration attitude that written prose must follow polite speech; pedantry and 'hard words' were to be left behind at college. Much of his writing, like *The Examiner*, was party journalism, in the tradition of Roger L'Estrange, that demanded immediate understanding. From different origins, Defoe came to much the same point. Political journalism was his metier for many years. His audience was lower in the social scale, and simplicity and clarity were even more necessary. For both, the 'literary' successes of *Gulliver* and *Robinson Crusoe* were relatively late, coming after years of the practice of what might be called applied prose, carefully designed for a specific audience that extended far beyond the well-educated.

Swift shows a professional's interest in his craft. His letter to the *Tatler* (No. 231, 1710) called for a middle style that avoids both the 'barbarity' of vulgar abbreviations and the 'abundance of poly-syllables'. His *Proposal for Correcting, Improving, and Ascertaining the English Tongue* (1712) advocated a society on the lines of the French Academy set up by Richelieu in 1635 and pleaded for the better education of what for him was the key group, the 'young nobility'. His fullest statement appeared in his *Letter to a Young Clergyman* (1719–20), where he stressed the importance of simplicity and condemned 'hard words'. As ideals he held up the Bible, the Prayer-Book, Bunyan, and the *Spectator*: 'Proper words in proper places makes the true definition of a style.'

Defoe, too, dreamed of a Richelieu-type academy, in his essay 'Of Academies', printed in his first major publication, *An Essay upon Several Projects* (1697). He saw its task as bringing 'our Gentlemen to a Capacity of Writing like themselves'. In terms strikingly like Swift's he excluded from his Academy 'meer Learned Men, and Graduates in the last Degree of Study, whose English has been far from Polite, full of Stiffness and Affectation, hard words, and long unusual couplings of Syllables and Sentences'. It was linguistic as much as political tact that suggested his membership:

> I wou'd therefore have this Society wholly compos'd of Gentlemen; whereof Twelve to be of the Nobility, if possible, and Twelve Private Gentlemen, and a Class of Twelve to be open to meer Merit.[7]

Perhaps fortunately, the various projects for an English Academy (which go back to Dryden and Royal Society days) came to nothing. The Restoration victory of the gentleman over the scholar was complete. English prose has never been written at such a high uniform level as when the coffee-house, the club, and the periodical reader provided the writer with an audience, literate but not learned, of whose response he was immediately aware. Addison was pre-eminently describing a code of writing, in his well-known claim:

> I have brought Philosophy out of Closets and Libraries, Schools and Colleges, to dwell in Clubs and Assemblies, at Tea-Tables and in Coffee-Houses.

> [*Spectator*, No. 10, 1711]

Much of the prose of this period is almost undisguised talk: Dryden in his various prefaces discusses his critical problems aloud; the *Spectator*, the *Tatler*, the *Guardian* and their successors take the reader into the writer's confidence; early fiction like *Gulliver* and *Robinson Crusoe* is written in the first person; the 'private' letter (penned generally with an eye to publication) has never been so well done – with Horace Walpole and Lady Mary Wortley Montagu it achieves the status of an art form. In a passage like the following, formal distinctions between conversation, letter, and essay are all but lost:

> I find, by Several Letters which I receive daily, that many of my Readers would be better pleased to pay Three Half-Pence for my Paper, than Two-Pence. The ingenious T. W. tells me, that I have deprived him of the best part of his Breakfast, for that, since the Rise of my Paper, he is forced every Morning to drink his Dish of Coffee by itself, without the Addition of the *Spectator*, that used to be better than Lace to it. *Eugenius* informs me very obligingly, that he never thought he should have disliked any Passage in my Paper, but that of late there have been two words in every one of them, which he could heartily wish left out, *viz. Price Two-Pence.* I have a letter from a Soap-Boyler ...

> [ADDISON, *Spectator*, No. 488, 1712]

The periodical essay of Addison and Steele was the major prose genre of the early eighteenth century. It was essentially a conversation, or at least one side of a conversation. The writer never forgets that there is another person present.

Even with topics, more specialised than the popular writing of the essayists, where the audience is necessarily limited, the prose of the period preserves the movement of intelligent conversation. Sociological writing, like Mandeville's *Fable of the Bees* (1714) and Shaftesbury's *Characteristics* (1711), the philosophical writings of Locke before 1700 and of Berkeley and Hume after that date, all move in simple sentence-structures, and are free from the jargon and professional vocabulary that was later to overwhelm much writing of this type. In the following examples, the authors all write, as is their custom, in the first person, and all (notably Berkeley) show a continuous awareness of the presence of a reader, who implicitly supplies the other half of the 'conversation':

> At Disasters, we either laugh, or pity those that befal them, according to the Stock we are possess'd of either Malice or Compassion. If a Man falls or hurts himself so slightly that it moves not the first, we laugh, and here our Pity and Malice shake us alternately: Indeed, Sir, I am very sorry for it, I beg your Pardon for laughing, I am the silliest Creature in the World, then laugh again; and again; I am indeed very sorry, and so on. Some are so Malicious that they would laugh if a Man broke his Leg, and others are so Compassionate that they can heartily Pity a Man for the least Spot in his Clothes; but nobody is so Savage that no Compassion can touch him, nor any man so good-natur'd as never to be affected with any Malicious Pleasure.[8]
>
> [MANDEVILLE, *The Fable of the Bees*, 1714]

> But, say you, the picture of a man is inverted, and yet the appearance is erect: I ask, what mean you by the picture of the man, or, which is the same thing, the visible man's being inverted? You tell me it is inverted because the heels are uppermost and the head undermost? Explain me this. You say, that by the head's being undermost, you mean that it is nearest to the earth, and by the heels being uppermost, that they are furthest from the earth. I ask again, what earth you mean? You cannot mean the picture of the earth that is painted on the eye ...[9]
>
> [G. BERKELEY, *An Essay towards a New Theory of Vision*, 1709]

> But suppose, that all the historians who treat of England, should agree, that, on the first of January 1600, Queen Elizabeth died; that both before and after her death she was seen by her physicians and the whole court, as is usual with persons of her rank; that her successor was acknowledged and proclaimed by the parliament; and that, after being interred a month, she again appeared, resumed the throne, and governed England for three years: I must confess I should be surprised at the concurrence of so many odd circumstances, but should not have the least inclination to believe so miraculous an event. I should not doubt of her pretended death, and of those other public circumstances that followed it: I should only assert it to have been pretended, and

that it neither was, nor possibly could be, real. You would in vain
object to me ...[10]

[D. HUME, *An Enquiry concerning Human Understanding*, 1748]

I think it is beyond question, that *Man has a clear perception of his own
Being*: he knows certainly, that he exists, and that he is something. He
that can doubt, whether he be anything, or no, I speak not to ...[11]

[LOCKE, *An Essay concerning Human Understanding*, 1690]

This 'polite' assumption that a reader is present, whose views are not to be
neglected, whose range of vocabulary must not be exceeded, and the utter
lack of the rhetorical clamour through which writers of the previous
century had demanded attention can yet produce works of devastating
effect. Berkeley coolly denies the evidence of our senses; Hume challenges
the assumptions of his age; both without raising the voice. Defoe
mercilessly dissects a mercantile society in *Crusoe* and *Moll Flanders* in
tradesman's talk; controlled passion lies just below the upper-class polite-
ness of Swift's *Modest Proposal* and *Tale of a Tub*; Richardson in *Clarissa*
handles real tragedy through the language of a girl. The effectiveness of
this kind of prose comes not from the noise it makes, but from deliberate
tension, the contrast between the ease of the utterance and the shock of the
ideas, so effortlessly slid into our minds.

Granted the general acceptance of this prose, which in the early part of
the century found its most general audience in the periodical essay, with
Addison as the acknowledged master, the way was open for the establishment of the novel. Human conduct in fiction was nothing new. What was
new in the novel was the absolute acceptance of normal lower and middle
class life as the setting for the serious portrayal of human relationships.
Many forces, literary, sociological, economic, and the rest, came together
in the 1740's to create the English novel. The combination would have
been without issue if it had not been supported by a speech-based prose
accepted by every literate member of society.

From the first-person narrative of Defoe and the letter-writing of the
age, it required only the genius of Richardson to take the final step of
writing (as a series of letters) *Pamela* (1740) and *Clarissa* (1748), minutely
observed renderings of thought and speech. From the accepted prose of his
age (after some useful apprentice years of writing for the stage) Fielding
created both the dialogue and the narrative sections of *Joseph Andrews*
(1742) and its successors. Fielding, like Addison, liked to talk to his readers,
and his regular 'conversations', written in the first person, are an extension
of the Addisonian essay:

My reader then is not to be surprised, if, in the course of this work, he shall find some chapters very short, and others altogether as long; some that contain only the time of a single day, others that comprise years; in a word, if my history sometimes seems to stand still, and sometimes to fly. For all which I shall not look on myself as accountable to any court of critical jurisdiction whatever: for as I am, in reality, the founder of a new province of writing, so I am at liberty to make what laws I please therein.

[*Tom Jones*, Book ii, Ch. i, 1749]

It is beyond the scope of this study to illustrate in detail the basic conversational mode of the novel. Extensive passages of both dialogue and narrative would be required. The texts are, fortunately, both familiar and accessible. The following will serve to illustrate the typical loose-knit but effective structures of the eighteenth-century narrative:

It was Mr. Allworthy's custom never to punish any one, not even to turn away a servant, in a passion. He resolved, therefore, to delay passing sentence on Jones till the afternoon.

The poor young man attended at dinner, as usual; but his heart was too much loaded to suffer him to eat. His grief too was a good deal aggravated by the unkind looks of Mr. Allworthy; whence he concluded that Western had discovered the whole affair between him and Sophia; but as to Mr. Blifil's story, he had not the least apprehension; for of much the greater part he was entirely innocent; and for the residue, as he had forgiven and forgotten it himself, so he suspected no remembrance on the other side. When dinner was over, and the servants departed, Mr. Allworthy began to harangue. He set forth, in a long speech, the many iniquities of which Jones had been guilty, particularly those which this day had brought to light; and concluded by telling him, That unless he could clear himself of the charge, he was resolved to banish him from his sight for ever.

[FIELDING, *Tom Jones*, Book vi, Ch. xi, 1749]

As the 1740's developed, there were some traces of other modes in the novel. Fielding and Smollett both use for comic purposes a more inflated way of writing, which owes nothing to current speech. Fielding carefully signals such changes of style in his chapter heads (the 'signals' are here italicised):

'In which, *after some very fine writing*, the history goes on ...'

[*Joseph Andrews*, Ch. viii, 1742]

A battle sung by the muse in the Homerican style, and *which none but the classical reader can taste.'*

[*Tom Jones*, Book iv, Ch. viii, 1749]

Smollett tends to a comic inflation of vocabulary that reads sometimes like a parody of Johnson:

> The cloth, consisting of a piece of an old sail, was instantly laid, covered with three plates, which, by the colour, I could with difficulty discern to be metal, and as many spoons of the same composition, two of which were curtailed in the handles, and the other abridged in the lip.

[*Roderick Random*, Ch. xxv, 1748]

This comic pomposity is a deliberate addition in both authors. The normal manner of Richardson and Fielding was to provide the basic prose for most of the novel-writing of the eighteenth and nineteenth century, and Fanny Burney, Jane Austen, and Thackeray (to name no others) remain heavily in their debt.

The change that overtook English prose in the 1760's has already been mentioned; it will be discussed in detail in the following chapter. The century of prose that began in 1660 was brought, almost officially, to an end, in a series of English grammars. There had been many earlier grammars, going back to the sixteenth century, largely handbooks of renaissance rhetoric. What distinguishes the grammarians of the 1760's from their predecessors is their awareness of the importance of sentence-structure. The important texts are: Joseph Priestley's *Rudiments of English Grammar*, 1761; Robert Lowth's *Short Introduction to English Grammar*, 1762; Lord Kames' *Elements of Criticism*, 1762; Thomas Sheridan's *Course of Lectures on Elocution*, 1763; and Hugh Blair's *Lectures on Rhetoric*, originally delivered about 1762 but not published till 1783.

Two features distinguish all these text-books, a return to Quintilian as a source and to the periodic sentence as an ideal; and a sustained attack on conversation as the basis of written prose. Blair says of one passage he is criticising:

> Though this elliptical style be intelligible, and is allowable in conversation and epistolary writing, yet, in all writings of a serious or dignified kind, it is ungraceful.[12]

[BLAIR, *Lectures on Rhetoric and Belles Lettres*, pub. 1783]

The result is that sentences, even phrases, of Addison and Swift are constantly cited, criticised, and then carefully 'corrected' and rewritten to eliminate the conversational looseness that had in fact been one of the main sources of their strength:

> *You was*, the Second Person Plural of the Pronoun placed in agreement with the First or Third Person Singular of the Verb, is an enormous Solecism; and yet Authors of the first rank have inadvertently fallen into it.[13]
>
> [LOWTH, *English Grammar*, 1762]

So Lowth, citing examples of this 'solecism' (which was good early eighteenth-century speech) from Addison, Pope, and Bolingbroke. Kames, citing Cicero and Quintilian in support of 'suspending the sense till the close of the period', proceeds to rewrite 'loose' sentences from *Spectator* and *Guardian*.[14] Blair complains of a sentence of Sir William Temple which contained eight 'ands', and corrects sentence after sentence of speech-based prose by Addison and Swift, removing conversational idiom, eliminating prepositions at the end of sentences, removing 'negligences', and hammering English prose into a new mould – he uses 'stately' and 'pompous' as terms of commendation.[15] The influence of these grammarians then and later has been profound. English 'grammar' has come from the grammarians, not from the writers of English prose. The grammatical doctrine of the 1760's, which drove a wedge between spoken and written prose, was brought together in popular form in 1795 in Lindley Murray's *English Grammar*, of which 200 editions were published before 1850.

It has been suggested by Professor James Sutherland[16] that this change to a stricter and more 'scholarly' prose was due to the growing numbers of influential Scottish writers, who as dialect speakers were out of touch with polite conversation in English – he notes Burke's comment on Robertson, that he wrote like a man 'who composes in a dead language which he understands but does not speak'. As a full explanation of the change I do not find Sutherland's argument convincing. Burke is here a suspect witness. He was himself a writer of the new baroque, and had no sympathy with the conversational mode of Swift and of Addison. The grammarians' attack on colloquial prose was not confined to Scots like Blair and Kames, and did not start with them. Priestley was a Yorkshireman, and Lowth (Bishop of Oxford and of London successively) was born at Winchester, an Oxford man and son of an Oxford don. His *Grammar* was the most influential of the group, at least ten editions appearing before Blair published his lectures. Blair called Lowth's book 'the grammatical performance of the highest authority that has appeared in our language'[17] and drew on both this and Priestley's *Grammar* as the source of his strictures on 'our best authors'. One must search further afield for the real causes of the change.

The 'century', 1660-1760, is the second of the great periods of English prose. In the previous hundred years, English had emerged as a prose medium capable of great and generally resonant writing. In this second hundred years the resonance was silenced, to be replaced by clarity, polite familiarity, ease of comprehension. This latter 'century' sees the beginnings of modern English prose. There are to be many variants in the next two hundred years. But it is difficult to avoid the conclusion that the years 1660-1760 set what was to remain the pattern, from which the variants are always seen *as* variants. The reader of today returns to the prose of this period, as of no other period, barely conscious of stepping back in time, because, once again, the written medium echoes faithfully the permanent speech-structures of the language.

Notes

1 w. s. LEWIS, ed., *Horace Walpole's Correspondence*, London, 1948, vol. 14, 137.
2 *Ibid.*
3 IAN WATT, *The Rise of the Novel*, London, 1957, Ch. 2.
4 H. DAVIS, ed., *Prose Works of Jonathan Swift*, Oxford, 1962, ix, 65, 'Letter to a Young Gentleman lately entered into Holy Orders'.
5 J. R. SUTHERLAND, ed., *Essays on the Eighteenth Century*, Oxford, 1945, 95, 'Some Aspects of Eighteenth Century Prose'.
6 H. MCLACHLAN, *English Education under the Test Acts*, Manchester, 1931, Appendix I.
7 S. I. TUCKER, *English Examined*, Cambridge, 1961, 60, Defoe 'of Academies'.
8 F. B. KAYE, ed., *Mandeville's The Fable of the Bees*, Oxford, 1924, 139-40.
9 A. C. FRASER, ed., *G. Berkeley's Works*, 1901, i, 183.
10 D. C. YALDEN-THOMSON, ed., *Hume's Theory of Knowledge*, London, 1951, 133.
11 LOCKE, *Essay concerning Human Understanding*, Bk. iv, Ch. x, s. 2.
12 HUGH BLAIR, *Lectures*, 1823 ed., i, 267.
13 S. I. TUCKER, *op. cit.*, 100, 'Lowth's *English Grammar*'.
14 H. KAMES, *Elements of Criticism*, Edinburgh, 1807 ed., ii, 76-7.
15 HUGH BLAIR, *Lectures*, (lecture xi, xii), 'The Structure of Sentences'; (lectures xx-xxiii), 'Critical Examination of the Style ... of the *Spectator*'; (lecture xxiv), 'Critical Examination of the Style ... of Dean Swift's Writings'.
16 SUTHERLAND, *op. cit.*, 107-8.
17 BLAIR, *op. cit.*, i, 211.

Chapter 14

The Reaction against Speech

1. The New Classical Prose

The movement of the 1760's away from a prose founded on polite speech was of some complexity, and two main changes of direction can be detected in the latter half of the eighteenth century. One represents the last major influence of renaissance-classical rhetoric and for this reason the term, the 'new classical prose', seems not inappropriate for the elaborate prose of Johnson, Gibbon, and Burke. The other was the beginnings, at first uncertain and only occasionally successful, of what was to become romantic prose. Each demands separate analysis.

Well before 1760 Johnson had established a manner of writing which ran counter to the prose of his contemporaries. 'Whoever wishes to attain an English style, familiar but not coarse, and elegant but not ostentatious, must give his days and nights to the volumes of Addison.' So runs one of his best-known critical comments on prose style. It needs careful reading. *Whoever*, in this comment, does not include Dr. Johnson. Johnson had no wish to attain a familiar English style. The well-known praise of Addison is, in its full context, tempered with cautions less often quoted: Addison's prose is the 'middle style'; it 'sometimes descends too much to the language of conversation'; its sentences lack 'studied amplitude'; its periods are not 'diligently rounded'. Johnson's whole instinct was towards a more formal prose, less involved with the reader, and the blend of neo-Quintilian rhetoric with heavily latinised vocabulary which he created had – Johnson being Johnson – a powerful influence on the style of serious writing in the second half of the century.

Johnson – and he was followed by Gibbon and Burke – abandoned the colloquial prose of his contemporaries because it was too slipshod and informal for his purposes. He set a deliberate distance between writer and recipient. The individual reader (be he philosopher or 'Soap-Boyler') who had silently supplied the other half of a 'conversation' with Berkeley or Addison is lost sight of, to be replaced by an impersonal audience, 'the public', or 'the common reader' or, often, simply 'the world'. A man 'in his transactions with the world', Johnson wrote in the first two paragraphs of the first *Rambler* (1750), needs some established ceremonial mode of entrance in presenting himself 'before the public'. 'I look with pleasure on my book', he wrote in the Preface to the *Dictionary* (1755), 'and deliver it to the world'. So Gibbon, in his first preface (1776), presumes to 'lay before the public' his initial volume; by the preface of 1781 he claimed he had abundantly discharged his 'engagements with the public'.

This deliberate loss of intimacy resulted in the creation of an impersonal prose which was self-consciously 'classical'. The new classical prose differed considerably from the prose of the earlier humanists. Johnson can never be mistaken for Milton, though both owe allegiance to Latin. Milton will follow where Cicero leads, even if it means wrenching the natural English order. Johnson avoids familiar style and 'low' language, but he cannot escape from a century of speech-based sentence-structure. With few exceptions, the ordering of his words and of his clauses is a natural speech order. Yet the total effect bears no resemblance to the polite speech of the time, because superimposed on the speech order are two major devices which dominate the Johnsonian sentence, a special vocabulary derived from Latin and a group of rhetorical figures derived from Quintilian.

The Johnsonian vocabulary had its source in his immense reading for the *Dictionary*. The key words of a sentence are 'translated' from a native to a classical form, from a short word to a long one. This process of translation can be seen literally in action in the scene recorded in Boswell's *Life*, where Johnson said of *The Rehearsal*, 'It has not wit enough to keep it sweet' and then immediately corrected himself by 'translating' the sentence into, 'It has not vitality enough to preserve it from putrefaction.' Johnson has begun with a speech-based sentence that could have been written by Swift. Leaving the structure and the word-order intact, he alters the entire effect by 'elevating' the words that carry the main speech-stresses into latinised words that continue to carry the stress but now demand extra attention because of their less familiar and more complex form. It is a mannerism only possible for a man with a feeling for the movement of speech and an immense 'classical' vocabulary within immediate reach.

That the elaborate classical vocabulary was a deliberate means of demanding attention is implied in his criticism of Swift's prose in his *Life of Swift*:

This easy and safe conveyance of meaning it was Swift's desire to attain, and for having attained he deserves praise, though perhaps not the highest praise. For purposes merely didactick, when something is to be told that was not known before, it is the best mode, but against that inattention by which known truths are suffered to lie neglected, it makes no provision; it instructs, but does not persuade.

Attention-demanding latinisms are such a feature of his prose that little illustration is necessary. Such still-remembered phrases as 'connubial infelicity' (*Rasselas*), 'cumbrous splendour' (*Life of Gray*), 'easy, vulgar, and therefore disgusting' (*Life of Milton*), 'where there is no emulation, there will be vanity' (*Life of Shenstone*) attest to their continuing power of capturing and retaining the interest of the reader.

Johnson's other devices for the avoidance of the mere 'easy and safe conveyance of meaning' are derived from the rhetoric of the humanists. His addiction to parallelism of words and phrases, to antitheses of words and clauses, to minor devices like alliteration and chiasmus, can be matched in any page of Lyly or Sidney, though the similarity is obscured by the abstract nature of Johnson's vocabulary. 'Retrenching exuberances and correcting inaccuracies', 'penury of knowledge and vulgarity of sentiment' (*Life of Pope*), 'His tragedy seems to be skill, his comedy to be instinct' (*Preface to Shakespeare*) are 'Euphuistic' structures that are repeated from his earliest prose to his latest.

From these elements Johnson built his unique but influential style. His normal sentence is lengthy, sometimes formally periodic, or if not periodic, the major emphasis comes late. To achieve this late emphasis, he adopts a device (recognisably 'Johnsonian') which runs counter to ordinary speech. Many of his sentences begin with a prepositional phrase or a noun clause which in speech would come after and not before the verb:

'That it will immediately become popular I have not promised to myself'

[Preface to the *Dictionary*]

Of the Epistle from 'Eloisa to Abelard', I do not know the date.

[*Life of Pope*]

The full combination of all these elements can best be seen in *The Rambler*, where Johnson is at his most exuberant, writing sentences 'diligently rounded' and of 'studied amplitude' that verge on the baroque:

With the same kind of anxious veneration I have for many years been making observations on the life of Polyphilus, a man whom all his acquaintances have, from his first appearance in the world, feared for the quickness of his discernment, and admired for the multiplicity of his attainments, but whose progress in life, and usefulness to mankind has been hindered by the superfluity of his knowledge, and the celerity of his mind.

[The *Rambler*, No. 19]

Gibbon in his great history (1776–81) had to find a prose style that would sustain a narrative through hundreds of pages. 'Many experiments were made before I could hit on the middle tone between a dull chronicle and a rhetorical declamation', he wrote afterwards in his *Autobiography*. The final result of his experiments was a uniformly elevated, 'classical', series of periodic sentences, the internal emphases of which depended on the Quintilian rhetoric which Johnson had re-established. Parallelism, antithesis, and the latinised word at the speech-stress remain the common features:

I was neither elated by the ambition of fame, nor depressed by the apprehension of contempt.

[*Autobiography*]

But the counsels of princes are more frequently influenced by views of temporal advantage than by considerations of abstract and speculative truth.

[*Decline and Fall*]

Instead of exposing his legions in the open plains of Mesopotamia, he advanced through the mountains of Armenia, where he found the inhabitants devoted to his cause, and the country as favourable to the operations of infantry as it was inconvenient for the motions of cavalry.

[*Decline and Fall*]

As the latter two examples show, Gibbon found these effects equally useful for comment and for narration. He avoided Johnson's often freakish pedantry, and the consistently dignified and distant tone – the reader held off at arm's length – admirably suited the scale of his work.

Burke, the third of this group of writers, does not so much adopt the new classical prose as encompass it. Balance, antithesis, and latinism – all this is second nature to him. He frequently adds, for good measure, epanaphora or 'like beginnings'. They are all present in a famous passage:

It is gone, that sensibility of principle, that chastity of honour, which felt a stain like a wound, which inspired courage while it mitigated ferocity, which enobled whatever it touched, and under which vice itself lost half its evil, by losing all its grossness.

[*French Revolution*]

But for all its rhetorical figures, this sentence (which is typical of the author) has reverted to a non-periodic pattern. Both in syntax and in speech-stress, the emphasis falls on the first three words, to which the remainder is an expansion. For Burke classical rhetoric is only part of the repertoire.

2. The Beginnings of Romantic Prose

Certain effects in Burke cannot be explained in terms of classical rhetoric:

Surely this is an awful subject; or there is none this side of the grave.

[*Conciliation with America*]

'This side of the grave' is a use of language which in earlier prose can be paralleled only in the Bible and some seventeenth-century sermon writers. Burke is calling on his reader to respond emotionally to the semantic overtones of language. Frequently he writes passages that have no parallel in any earlier prose:

Seas roll, and months pass, between the order and the execution; and the want of a speedy explanation of a single point is enough to defeat a whole system. You have, indeed, winged ministers of vengeance, who carry your bolts in their pounces to the remotest verge of the sea. But there a power steps in, that limits the arrogance of raging passions and furious elements, and says, 'So far shalt thou go, and no farther.'

[*Conciliation with America*]

Prose of this type became so common in the nineteenth century that it requires an adjustment of mind to accept that in the late eighteenth century something quite new was being created, a prose directed towards manipulating the feelings of the reader. Burke was, of course, an orator, but this manipulation was not confined to oratory. Two devices through which Burke achieves his effects – the use of evocative imagery and of a sentence made up of short co-ordinated elements – are the common property of a group of his contemporaries, notably the writers of the sentimental and terror novel.

In the prose of the previous two centuries it is most unusual to find an appeal other than to the reader's reason; even prose of persuasion like *Areopagitica* uses metaphor and simile mainly as illustrative parallels to what is conceived as a continuous set of reasoned arguments. Burke, too, argues; but he reinforces his rational arguments with bold, evocative, imagery that operates on the reader at a sub-conscious level. 'Seas roll', 'winged ministers', 'the remotest verge of the sea' anticipate the language of Coleridge and Shelley and Byron. The prose-writer is moving into what had up till now been a linguistic province of the poet, and the poet's emotionally toned imagery is frequent in prose after 1760:

> In a moment she heard the step of some person. Her blood curdled.
>
> [WALPOLE, *The Castle of Otranto*, 1764]

> The sun looked bright in the morning after, to every eye in the village but Le Fever's and his afflicted son's; the hand of death pressed heavy upon his eye-lids, – and hardly could the wheel at the cistern turn round its circle.
>
> [STERNE, *Tristram Shandy*, Book vi, Chap. x, 1762]

> The still air seemed scarcely to breathe upon the woods, and now and then the distant sound of a solitary sheep-bell, or of a closing casement, was all that broke the silence.
>
> [RADCLIFFE, *The Mysteries of Udolpho*, 1794]

Skill in the use of such evocative imagery varies. Walpole's 'her blood curdled', an image from the Elizabethan dramatists, was already on the way to becoming a cliché. Burke handles his images with great sensitivity. Sterne uses emotionally toned imagery effectively, but sparingly; his reasons for caution are Shandean:

> The highest stretch of improvement a single word is capable of, is a high metaphor, – for which, in my opinion, the idea is generally the worse, and not the better.
>
> [*Tristram Shandy*, Book v, Ch. xlii, 1762]

Prose, written as a succession of 'high metaphors', came to be a notable feature of the early nineteenth century. It was to have its own successes; and its own dangers. Its origins are firmly set in the 1760's – the decade of Percy's *Reliques*, *Fingal*, Shenstone's *Miscellany*, Hurd's *Letters on Chivalry and Romance*, and Chatterton. The new emotional toning of prose was part of a general shift in sensibility.

The task set by the originators of romantic prose was to find ways of writing which would communicate excited feeling. Pathos, terror, and warm sentiment, they discovered, could be induced by syntax, through variations in the sentence-structure. A favourite device was the series of short sentences, either in parataxis or in simple co-ordination:

> The blood and spirits of Le Fever, which were waxing cold and slow within him, and were retreating to their last citadel, the heart – rallied back, – the film forsook his eyes for a moment, – he looked up wishfully in my uncle Toby's face, – then cast a look upon his boy, – and that ligament, fine as it was, – was never broken.–
>
> Nature instantly ebbed again, – the film returned to its place, – the pulse fluttered, – stopped – went on – throbbed – stopped again – moved – stopped – shall I go on? – No.
>
> [*Tristram Shandy*, Book vi, Ch. x, 1762]

This manner became almost standardised for the pathos of a death scene with the sentimental novelists:

> Had you seen us, Mr. Hartley, when we were turned out of South-hill, I am sure you would have wept at the sight. You remember old Trusty, my shag house-dog; I shall never forget it while I live; the poor creature was blind with age, and could scarce crawl after us to the door; he went however as far as the gooseberry-bush; that you may remember stood on the left side of the yard; he was wont to bask in the sun there; when he had reached that spot, he stopped; we went on: I called to him; he wagged his tail, but did not stir: I called again; he lay down: I whistled, and cried Trusty; he gave a short howl, and died!
>
> [H. MACKENZIE, *The Man of Feeling*, 1771]

Seventy years later Dickens can still use the manner for a more famous death-scene, confident that his readers from the simplest serving-maid to Lord Jeffrey will respond with tears:

> For she was dead. There, upon her little bed, she lay at rest. The solemn stillness was no marvel now.
>
> [*The Old Curiosity Shop*, Ch. lxxi, 1841]

Sterne, in particular, is an innovator in syntax. *Tristram Shandy* is in the form of a sequence of conversations with occasional monologues. At first glance it might seem to belong to the tradition of speech-based written prose of the seventeenth and the eighteenth centuries. But a closer examination suggests that Sterne ignores most of the previously accepted patterns of speech-based sentence-structure. What he is trying to reproduce is not the movement of speech but of thought. All the characters of *Tristram Shandy* are overheard thinking aloud – they seldom listen to one another – and what passes for conversation is generally a series of virtually interior monologues, arranged by Sterne as a kind of syntactical counterpoint for several voices. Sterne's 'sentences' are neither those of classical rhetoric nor of 'written' polite conversation. They are often made up of a string of statements, clauses, phrases, single words, parentheses and exclamations, designed to transcribe the 'pre-grammatical' sequences of free association:

> The verbs auxiliary we are concerned in here, continued my father, are, am; was; have; had; do; did; made; suffer; shall; should; will; would; can; could; owe; ought; used; or is wont. – And these varied with tenses, present, past, future, and conjugated with the verb see, – or with these questions added to them: – Is it? Was it? Will it be? Would it be? May it be? Might it be? And these again put negatively, Is it not? Was it not? Ought it not? – Or affirmatively, – It is; It was; It ought to be. Or chronologically, – Has it been always? Lately? How long ago? – Or hypothetically, – If it was? If it was not? What would follow? – If the French should beat the English? If the Sun go out of the Zodiac?
>
> [*Tristram Shandy*, Book v, Ch. xliii, 1762]

By the end of the eighteenth century English prose settled into what for all but a few eccentrics has proved to be its modern form. Three 'styles' had been evolved and these have remained the basis for virtually all later writers. First, there was what can well be claimed as the central tradition, the speech-based prose that had been perfected between 1660 and 1760, to which the present-day reader can return with little fear of meeting archaism or obsolescence. He responds readily to the still familiar movement of the language. So too, in the nineteenth century, did Jane Austen, Hazlitt, Newman, Thackeray, who continued to write in speech-based structures, with the minimum of metaphoric heightening.

Secondly, there was the prose of neo-Quintilian rhetoric, which was to provide the model for most 'serious' writing in the nineteenth century; what Sir Walter Scott (contrasting himself with Jane Austen) called 'the Big Bow-Wow strain': the criticism of the *Edinburgh Review*; the 'literature' of economics, philosophy, and the expanding physical sciences; the ubiquitous text-book; the newspaper leader. At its best, it was a useful medium for accurate exposition. But it demands a parity of background between writer and reader. Unlike speech-based prose, unless it is carefully controlled it degenerates easily into excess. The educated have not always written it well; and the ill-educated, over whom it sometimes exercises a fatal fascination, have always written it badly. It has remained the source of much prose of dubious acceptability.

Finally, there was the prose which I have called romantic, though its limits extend well beyond any normal definition of the romantic period. In contradistinction to the two other styles, it is marked by the continuous use of syntactical and metaphoric devices designed to excite an affective response. Defined in these terms, romantic prose extends from its beginnings in the 1760's through the writers of the romantic period proper like Lamb and De Quincey, to later nineteenth-century writers like Pater and Ruskin and Hardy, and twentieth-century writers like Joyce and D. H. Lawrence. Of the three, it has in the past century and a half been subjected to the greatest degree of variation and experiment. The process is still going on, with the result that the criteria by which one may judge romantic prose are still not easy to determine.

Some attempt will be made in the ensuing chapter to trace the later usage of these three styles and to explore what appear to be their more important developments.

Chapter 15

The Shaping of Modern Prose: Non-fiction

Modern prose can be reasonably dated from the early years of the nineteenth century, when a milieu was established that has not in essence altered since. The notable feature, which distinguishes the nineteenth and the twentieth from all previous centuries, is the massive expansion of the reading public. In the earliest centuries, when prose was oral, 'reading' had meant 'reading aloud', and the 'non-reader' was a listener at no serious disadvantage. Indeed his presence had influenced and shaped both secular and religious prose in the Middle Ages and the early renaissance years. Paradoxically, it was Caxton and his successors who put him at a disadvantage; by the early sixteenth century, 'reading' had acquired its modern visual sense. Though the easy multiplication of the printing press brought this new conception of reading within reach of greater numbers, print at the same time became a barrier that cut off the largest segment of English society from literature increasingly conceived in terms of the printed book. Between 1500 and 1800 the humble (and non-literate) majority took no part in the shaping of English prose. They did not read; and the speech-based prose that emerged was not based on their speech.

There had, of course, always been a modestly increasing degree of literacy at the base of the social pyramid. The nineteenth century saw for the first time a concerted, and in the long term successful, effort to make readers of the labouring poor in the country and the industrial towns. The educational writings of the Edgeworths, the technique of class instruction associated with Bell and Lancaster, the growth from the late eighteenth century of Sunday schools, the establishment in 1811 of the National Society for Promoting the Education of the Poor, and in 1814 of its rival the British and Foreign School Society led by 1833 to the first parliamentary grant for elementary education and ultimately to the Act of 1870. By the end of the nineteenth century the printed word was open to all.

The process was speeded by the technological advances of the time. Up till the end of the eighteenth century, Caxton would have found little in a London printing house that was unfamiliar. After 1800, his ghost would have retreated in dismay. Earl Stanhope's newly invented press had increased the ease of hand printing. In 1814, steam not human muscle was in control in the printing house. Short cuts were common in the composing room: the eighteenth-century development of stereotyping was extensively used for cheap reprints; mechanical setting and finally the introduction of the linotype in 1889 ensured an avalanche of print.[1] The output was enormous, and was matched by a conspicuous consumption of a kind undreamt of by the inventor of the phrase.

It becomes increasingly difficult as one approaches modern times to think of prose (as one can for earlier periods) in terms of a reading public. There was a whole spectrum of reading publics, separated by differences in education and social status. Initially at least, the reading publics were distinguished by their ability to pay. The group who could lay out a guinea and a half for a new three-volume novel (or several guinea subscriptions to a circulating library) and six shillings for an issue of the *Edinburgh Review* forms one end of the spectrum. At the other were the earnest members of Mechanics' Institutes who with the blessing of the Society for the Diffusion of Useful Knowledge were by the 1830's buying Knight's *Penny Magazine* and *Penny Encyclopedia*. Cheap reprints bridged the gap; and it was further closed in the late thirties when Dickens began the practice of publishing novels in shilling monthly numbers. By the end of the century newspapers were selling for a halfpenny, and a large range of standard English authors from a penny to sixpence.

Modern prose is based on the three eighteenth-century codes, modified by the pressures that developed from writers and from this expanded and diversified reading public. The central speech-based prose continued to provide a norm, and for writers like Hazlitt and Arnold it was the staple way of writing. But the two variants underwent vigorous development during the nineteenth century. In sheer bulk of printed matter, they dominate the whole period. The general impression one carries away from extended reading in the non-fictional prose of the time is certainly not that of direct simplicity.

What in the later eighteenth century had been the tentative beginnings of romantic prose asserted itself early in the nineteenth century and in the current climate of individualism produced a whole range of mutations, the extremest form of which was a prose of display where (to repeat Bacon's caution in *The Advancement of Learning*) once more 'men began to hunt more after words than matter'.

The third code, the Johnsonian-latinised, continued, as could have been foreseen, as a medium for the discussion of the 'serious' topic. But it had a further development, which could not have been expected from its origins. The newly literate readers of the nineteenth century had no experience of the 'polite' speech which formed the basis of the central prose of earlier years. For them simplicity and directness were suspect – education should surely produce something more ambitious than their own limited vocabulary and speech patterns. For the newly literate, the prose that descended from Johnson appeared more 'educated' than the prose that descended from Addison. The result is that much 'popular' nineteenth-century prose, even in newspapers and novels and at the 'penny magazine' level, affected an elaboration of vocabulary and sentence-structure that today sounds absurdly pompous:

> 'Wretch!' exclaimed Julia, her countenance lighted up with contempt. 'Wretch! Too insignificant for my anger! Know that I despise your threats equally with your promises! And did I but possess the means of acquainting Lord Tremaine with your insolence, the chastisement which you so justly merit should quickly be your reward: but it is your machinations, and those of your sister, whose dishonour you you are so willing to hide, by accomplishing mine, that I am indebted for the deprivation of a husband's protecting arm ...'[2]

Serious Prose

The founders of the *Edinburgh Review* (1802) and of its rival the *Quarterly Review* (1809) discovered that there was a large audience prepared to welcome an intelligent and serious appraisal of the intellectual issues of the day. Though both journals are now usually remembered only for their literary articles (the *Edinburgh* on *The Excursion*; the *Quarterly* on *Endymion*), literary criticism occupied relatively few pages in any number. Politics, economics, travel and exploration, mathematics and the sciences, the world of affairs predominated. The audience was educated – 'No genteel family can pretend to be without the *Edinburgh Review*', wrote Sir Walter Scott when he was establishing the *Quarterly*. Together, the journals provided a forum for long articles from writers of the calibre of Jeffrey, Macaulay, Southey and Scott, and established a tone and style for the discussion of serious topics that persisted through the entire century.

The advertisement to the first issue of the *Edinburgh* reveals at the outset the source of the prose:

> Of the books that are daily presented to the world, a very large proportion is evidently destined to obscurity, by the insignificance of their subjects, or the defects of their execution: and it seems unreasonable to expect that the Public should be interested by any account of performances, which have never attracted any share of its attention.

The inverted order of the opening prepositional phrase, the 'world', the 'Public', the antithesis and balance, the Latin abstractions are unmistakeable Johnsonian hallmarks. It would be claiming too much to suggest that Johnson is the only influence – Jeffrey started a well-known article on Wordsworth with the cry, 'This will never do!' But the long, often periodic, sentence with rhetorical 'figures' and latinisms forms the basis of the prose of both journals, which (consciously or unconsciously) imposed this style on their contributors, even when they wrote quite otherwise for a different audience. Scott, who in other contexts was a writer of romantic prose, wrote for the *Quarterly* in Johnsonian phrases ('conjugal machinations', 'solitary celibacy') and in Quintilian-type figures:

> There can be no doubt that, by the studied involution and extrication of the story, by the combination of incidents, new, striking, and wonderful beyond the course of ordinary life, the former authors opened that obvious and strong sense of interest which arises from curiosity; as by the pure, elevated, and romantic cast of the sentiment, they conciliated those better propensities of our nature which loves to contemplate the picture of virtue even when confessedly unable to imitate its excellences.
>
> [Review of *Emma*, *Quarterly Review*, October 1815]

The influence of this prose is everywhere apparent. With few exceptions, the philosopher, the historian, the physical and social scientist of the last century, even in his moments of conscious popularising, tends to the vocabulary and the sentence structure of Johnsonian prose and not to the 'native easiness' and 'mathematical plainness' of his seventeenth-century edecessor:

> This knowledge, as Aristotle held, might be permanently precluded by vicious habits, or temporarily obliterated by passion ...
>
> [HENRY SIDGWICK, Ethics, *Encyclopedia Britannica*, 9th ed., 1875]

> I had now learnt by experience that the passive susceptibilities need to be cultivated as well as the active capacities, and require to be nourished and enriched as well as guided.
>
> [J. S. MILL, *Autobiography*, 1873]

As soon as some ancient member in the great series of the Primates came to be less arboreal, owing to a change in its manner of procuring subsistence, or to some change in the surrounding conditions, its habitual manner of progression would have been modified; and thus it would have been rendered more strictly quadrupedal or bipedal.

[c. DARWIN, *The Descent of Man*, 1871]

The better writers of general prose of the present century have moved away from this way of writing. Yet it persists in some areas of expositional and scientific prose, sometimes degenerating into mere jargon. Serious writing, particularly on topics which necessarily deal with abstract ideas, calls for a technical vocabulary, for which Latin and to a lesser extent Greek have proved to be the best sources. But even today, the dividing line between legitimate technicality and abstraction, and mere inflation of the type affected by a newly literate audience, is too frequently crossed.[3] The long shadows of Quintilian and Dr Johnson still lie heavily on much modern prose.

Romantic Prose

While the reviews were setting the tone for the serious reading of 'genteel families' (and their less genteel imitators) an even wider audience was being developed by the magazines, the best known of which were *Blackwood's Magazine* (founded 1817), the *London Magazine* (1820), Leigh Hunt's numerous journals like the *Indicator* (1819) and *Fraser's Magazine* (1830). In these periodicals fiction, the essay and belles-lettres provided an extensive literature of entertainment for which romantic prose was the accepted medium from the outset. Many of its landmarks first appeared in their pages – *The Essays of Elia* and the first version of *Confessions of an English Opium Eater* in the *London Magazine*, *Sartor Resartus* in *Fraser's*, the beginnings of Hogg's *Confessions of a Justified Sinner* in *Blackwood's*.

In the prose of the magazines, the now established conventions of the period, the gentleman conversing with gentleman, or the educated with the educated, were openly abandoned. *Blackwood* reviewing Lamb's works in 1818 frankly sneered at 'that dull or stupid prosing that weighs down the dying *Edinburgh Review*', and praised Lamb's style in a series of metaphors and evocative images that came to be a substitute for criticism during much of the nineteenth century:

He diverges into green lanes and sunshiny glades, and not seldom
into the darker and more holy places of undiscovered solitude.
[*Blackwood's Magazine*, August, 1818]

The writer of romantic prose has quite different aims from those of his
predecessors. He is not attempting to secure the co-operation of his audience by using their normal language; nor is he trying to convince them
by appealing to a shared (or ostensibly shared) intellectual background. His
prose continually asserts his personal individuality, his uniqueness; and
the emotionally affected audience is expected to respond not so much
with comprehension as with astonished admiration. As a result, the metaphor, the emotionally toned image, disrupted exclamatory and staccato
syntax and the Sterne-type monologue provide a basic formula that is
repeated with many personal variations:

> With other eyes, too, could I now look upon my fellow man; with
> an infinite Love, with an infinite Pity. Poor, wandering, wayward
> man! Art thou not tried, and beaten with stripes, even as I am?
> Ever, whether thou bear the royal mantle or the beggar's gabardine,
> art thou not so weary, so heavy laden; and thy Bed of Rest is but a
> Grave. O my Brother, my Brother ...
>   [CARLYLE, *Sartor Resartus*, *Fraser's Magazine*, 1834]

> Ah, hasten, while yet it is of use to haste; ere yet the spotty horror
> fixes on the nap! Out with the protecting handkerchief, which, tied
> round the hat, and flowing off in a corner behind, shall gleam through
> the thickening night like a suburb comet!
>   [L. HUNT, 'A Chapter on Hats', *The Indicator*, 1819]

> She took, and gave, no concessions. She hated favours. She never
> made a revoke, nor ever passed it over in her adversary without
> exacting the utmost forfeiture. She fought a good fight: cut and
> thrust. She held not her good sword (her cards) 'like a dancer'. She
> sate bolt upright ...
>   [LAMB, 'Mrs. Battle's Opinion on Whist', *London Magazine*, 1821]

As the nineteenth century proceeded, romantic prose tended to become
more rather than less mannered, and evolved with writers like Stevenson
and Pater into a self-conscious prose of display. The change is particularly
notable in De Quincey. He revised his 1821 *Opium Eater* from the *London
Magazine* to the fully orchestrated version of 1856, and his later contributions to *Blackwood's Magazine*, the *Suspiria de Profundis* of 1845 and *The*

English Mail-Coach and *Dream-Fugue* of 1849, represent the ultimate in what De Quincey called, with his own and his audience's approbation, 'impassioned prose':

> Lo, it is summer, almighty summer! The everlasting gates of life and summer are thrown wide open; and on the ocean, tranquil and verdant as a savannah, the unknown lady from the dreadful vision and I myself are floating: she upon a fairy pinnace, and I upon an English three-decker. But both of us are wooing gales of festal happiness within the domain of our common country – within that ancient watery park – within that pathless chase where England takes her pleasure as a huntress through winter and summer, and which stretches from the rising to the setting sun. Ah! what a wilderness of floral beauty was hidden, or was suddenly revealed, upon the tropic islands through which the pinnace moved ...
>
> [DE QUINCEY, 'Dream-Fugue', *Blackwood's Magazine*, 1849]

Prose of this type, which has taken over the function and some of the techniques of the romantic lyric, was highly regarded in the nineteenth century. Today it seems almost an alien tongue in any serious literary context – though it continues with unabated vigour an extra-literary life in the special world of advertising. The writing of romantic prose rests on a perilous balance. Designed predominantly, sometimes exclusively, to affect an emotional response from the reader, it is peculiarly susceptible to shifts in sensibility. Certainly, the self-contained exercises in the genre (notably the essay, the dream, the 'purple passage') have not retained their hold on the modern reader. On the other hand, romantic prose written in an appropriate context of a longer work can have on occasion an extreme effectiveness. This is particularly so in the novel. Out of context, the end of *Wuthering Heights*, The Tom-all-Alone chapter (xlvi) of *Bleak House*, some of the descriptive passages of *The Horse's Mouth*, may seem overblown. In the full setting, where the narrative has built up the necessary tension, the imagery and the quasi-rhapsodical structures arrest the attention and ensure an adequate response.

Speech-based Prose

While the elaboration of latinised and romantic writing attracted considerable audiences, both educated and half-educated, some notable nineteenth-century writers of general prose resisted, and even for a 'magazine' audience preserved the eighteenth-century link between intelligent

conversation and written style. Temperamentally there was no close affilia-
tion between Hazlitt and Newman, Newman and Arnold. Yet Newman
learned from Hazlitt and Arnold from Newman. All three were speakers
before they were writers, Hazlitt as a public lecturer, Newman as a
preacher, and Arnold as Professor of Poetry. Much of their published
work was originally spoken before an audience and given only the
slightest revision for magazine or book publication in such volumes as
Characters of Shakespeare's Plays (1817), *Scope and Nature of University Education* (1853) and *Essays in Criticism* (1865). Even when there was no prior
spoken form – Newman's *Apologia* was written in a few weeks in 1864
for immediate pamphlet publication, and 'every page seems as if it were
rather spoken than written'[4] – the structures of speech and limits of
good-mannered conversation shape everything they write.

Hazlitt formulated his practice in an essay, 'On familiar Speech', published in his 1821-2 collection of *Table-Talk*. In an uncompromising defence of speech-based prose he attacked Johnson's 'tall, opaque words' and
echoed – perhaps unconsciously – Spratt's defence of 1667:

> To write a genuine familiar or truly English style is to write as any one
> would speak in common conversation who had a thorough command
> and choice of words, or who could discourse with ease, force, and
> perspicuity, setting aside all pedantic and oratorical flourishes.

A parallel attack on oratorical flourishes was made by Arnold in an Oxford
lecture of 1864. This lecture was shortly afterwards printed (in its spoken
form) for the magazine audience in the *Cornhill Magazine* and then became
the second section, 'The Literary Influence of Academies', of his 1865
volume, *Essays in Criticism*. The authors Arnold selects for his attack are
significant: Jeremy Taylor, the master of the baroque, and Burke, the
initiator of romantic prose:

> I say that is extravagant prose: prose too much suffered to indulge its
> caprices; prose at too great a distance from the centre of good taste;
> prose, in short, with a note of provinciality. People may reply, it is
> rich and imaginative; yes, that is just it, it is *Asiatic* prose, as the ancient
> critics would have said; prose somewhat barbarously rich and over-
> loaded. But the true prose is Attic prose.

Against such extravagance and overloaded richness, Arnold sets up his
own ideal, 'prose of the centre', essentially the spoken language of intelligent urban society, best represented in his own century by Newman and
in the eighteenth century by Addison.

One must recognise that Arnold and his supporters were in their day minority voices. The more elaborate types of prose heavily predominate in the whole period. They can still be found. But the present century has been one of these apparently inevitable times of adjustment when the whole movement of non-fictional prose has once more reverted to the base of speech. Romantic prose could be found in reputable journals as late as the 1920's. Today it is mainly confined to lower-grade fiction and advertising. Excessive latinity and Quintilian rhetoric survive in certain contexts, including what is sometimes called 'official' prose. But even here, it has been under massive assault and would appear to be in retreat. As one turns over the pages of Shaw's prefaces, the philosophical writings of Bertrand Russell, the critical essays of Eliot, it is difficult to avoid the conclusion that the English prose of the major writers in this century has returned to the main line.

Notes

1   E. HOWE, *The London Compositor*, London, 1947, 62–8.
2   M. DALZIEL, *Popular Fiction 100 Years Ago*, London, 1957, 28.
3   For a scientist's reservations concerning the English of modern scientific papers, see J. R. Baker in *Nature*, Nov. 1955, 851.
4   W. H. HUTTON, *Cambridge History of English Literature*, Cambridge, 1933, xii, 269, 'The Oxford movement'.

Chapter 16

The Shaping of Modern Prose: the Novel

It was, pre-eminently, in the novel that speech-based prose established its ascendancy. A full discussion of the complex usage of prose in the novel would call for a whole book in itself, and a short chapter on some salient points must suffice. Viewed (so to speak) anatomically, a novel consists of four prose 'systems': dialogue, narrative, description, and commentary. In many twentieth-century novels, the systems over-lap and run together, and a fifth system has been evolved, but this is a comparatively late development in the novel. In an eighteenth-century novel like *Tom Jones*, and generally in Fielding's successors – Scott, Dickens, Thackeray – the four systems are separate, and each could be written in a separate manner; as a result, each system (to continue the anatomical metaphor) can be dissected out and examined in isolation.

Dialogue – one need look no further than Jane Austen – consistently echoes the accepted speech of the day. A real life Elizabeth Bennet or Captain Wentworth would have used precisely the vocabulary and the sentence-structures that they display in Jane Austen's pages. But the range of speech in the novel has always been wider than the 'gentleman's agreement' which formed the speech-base of general prose. From its beginnings in Bunyan and Defoe, dialogue in the novel has attempted to reproduce the movement of conversation in a variety of regional accents and on different social levels.

This possibility of an extended speech-range has had important consequences. It has enabled the novel, within the covers of one book appealing to a wide range of readers, to be a medium of popular recreation and simultaneously to be a serious literary genre. The novel for two centuries now has remained the dominant literary form because it has retained the allegiance of a continually expanding reading public without thereby of necessity suffering any loss of serious intention. Not all novelists have accepted the full possible range or the full audience. The various levels of linguistic and syntactic sophistication represented by Joyce, Virginia Woolf, and James have explored the marginal possibilities of the novel without expectation of a popular following. Successful alterations in technique, however, in no way reduce the high critical estimate one must continue to place on the less complicated prose of (say) Dickens or Defoe. Sam Weller is as 'serious' a character as Stephen Dedalus, and *Moll Flanders* remains a more important novel than *Mrs Dalloway*.

For the individual novelist, the advantages of the extended speech-range have been considerable. It has enabled him to transcend the limits of his immediate milieu in a way inconceivable for the earlier writer of prose exclusively based on polite speech. Addison, perforce, must confine himself to Sir Roger and the Spectator Club. Fielding and Smollett, through their use of dialect and uneducated speech, can extend their sympathies (and the sympathies of their readers) to Squire Western and Winifred Jenkins. The lead once given, the way was open for Maria Edgeworth's Irish retainers, Scott's dialect-speaking farmers and lawyers, Mark Twain's America, and the later chorus of English provincial voices in George Eliot, Hardy, Lawrence, and the writers of our own day.

Narrative, on the other hand, has been written almost exclusively on the basis of educated speech – the writer tends to identify himself with the more educated of his audience, and the voice of the author as narrator is indistinguishable from his authentic voice as it can be heard in (e.g.) Thackeray's letters or Trollope's *Autobiography*. This led in the nineteenth century to some technical problems of presentation. Scott gave the entire narrative to a dialect speaker in Wandering Willie's Tale in *Redgauntlet*. But this is exceptional. Where the narrator is a persona other than the author, the general solution until quite recently has been to retain the author's voice, whether or not it is intrinsically appropriate: in *Wuthering Heights*, there are two servants, Joseph, and Nellie Dean. Joseph is clearly placed in his setting through dialect:

> There's nobbut t'missis, and shoo'll not oppen't an ye mak' yer flay-
> some dins till neeght.

Nellie Dean, formerly the maidservant, is, by the opening of the novel, the housekeeper; there is no suggestion that she is superior in education to Joseph or less provincial. But, since she carries the main task of narration, her narrative style, is, in fact, the formalised speech of her creator:

> So, from the very beginning, he bred bad feeling in the house; and at
> Mrs. Earnshaw's death, which happened in less than two years after,
> the young master had learned to regard his father as an oppressor
> rather than a friend, and Heathcliff as a usurper of his parent's affec-
> tions and his privileges.

The third prose system in the novel, the description of background and scenery, owes a great deal to the terror novel. Before the 1760's it was the poet rather than the prose-writer who was expected to have an eye for 'landskips', and the earlier novelists like Defoe and Fielding establish their settings in a few business-like sentences without emotional overtones. The terror novelists began what was to become a major element in the novel, the exploitation of setting and scenery to evoke atmosphere and mood. Horace Walpole's midnight scenes and Mrs. Radcliffe's forests and gloomy castles lead in turn to the innumerable full-scale landscapes of Scott, the wild and menacing moor and heath of the Brontës and Hardy, the fog-scape of *Bleak House* and the marshes of *Great Expectations*. For these passages, the short-winded syntactic structures and evocative imagery of romantic prose have since the 1760's been the accepted style:

> Here a few half withered trees hung from the crevices of the rock, and gave a picturesque wilderness to the object; there, clusters of half seen cottages, rising from among tufted groves, embellished the green margin of a stream which meandered in the bottom, and bore its waves to the blue and distant main.
>
> [MRS. RADCLIFFE, *The Italian*, 1797]

> Fog everywhere. Fog up the river, where it flows among the green aits and meadows; fog down the river, where it rolls defiled among the tiers of shipping, and the water-side pollutions of a great (and dirty) city. Fog on the Essex marshes, fog on the Kentish heights . . .
>
> [DICKENS, *Bleak House*, 1852]

> Who can say of a particular sea that it is old? Distilled by the sun, kneaded by the moon, it is renewed in a year, in a day, or in an hour. The sea changed, the fields changed, the rivers, the villages, and the people changed, yet Egdon remained.
>
> [HARDY, *The Return of the Native*, 1878]

Jane Austen protested: Marianne in chapter 16 of *Sense and Sensibility* rhapsodises on landscape in a mild parody of romantic prose, and the down-to-earth Edgar two chapters later responds with an attack on romantic imagery. But Jane Austen's protests went unheeded. English novelists, to the present century (and the 'realists' are not exempt), lean heavily on the romantic code of prose-writing in their passages of description:

> A great ship! For ages had the ocean battered in vain her enduring sides; she was there when the world was vaster and darker, when the sea was great and mysterious, and ready to surrender the prize of fame

to audacious men. A ship mother of fleets and nations! The great flag-
ship of the race; stronger than the storms! and anchored in the open
sea.

[CONRAD, *Nigger of the Narcissus*, 1897]

Yet the downs, in magnificent indifference, bearing limbs and body
to the sun, drinking sunshine and sea-wind and sea-wet cloud into its
golden skin, with superb stillness and calm of being, was not the downs
still more wonderful?

[LAWRENCE, *The Rainbow*, 1915]

The beetles had disappeared; the rain had apparently washed them
away; it came perpendicularly down, with a sort of measured intensity, as if it were driving nails into a coffin-lid.

[G. GREENE, *The Power and the Glory*, 1940]

The fourth prose system is commentary. There has been a variety of procedures, and prose usage has varied accordingly. Till late in the nineteenth
century the normal device was the appearance of the novelist in his own
pages (on his own stage, so to speak) as commentator and discursive mor-
alist. There is very frequently a sharp change in vocabulary and sentence
structure between narration and commentary. As narrator, the novelist is
merely telling a tale, in their own terms, to an audience of his peers. As
commentator, he assumes a persona, moralising, sermonising, registering
commendation or distaste for what he portrays. Even the normally self-
effacing Richardson at the conclusion of a letter by Pamela (Letter xxxi) –
which has closed on the colloquial note 'Well, no more – I'm in a fearful
hurry' – intervenes in a quite different prose:

Thus every way was the poor virgin beset; and the whole will shew
the base arts of designing men, to gain their wicked ends; and how
much it behoves the fair sex to stand upon their guard against artful
contrivances, especially when riches and power conspire against inno-
cence and a low estate.

When the novel abandoned the letter device in the 1740's, there was no
technical reason why the novelist should not be in his own novel, Fielding
for whole chapters, Dickens and Thackeray for substantial passages, and
many novelists (Trollope is a good example) for a sentence or interpolated
phrase. Fielding here gave the lead: the tone is often elevated (and both
serious and ironical elevation are possible), the syntax exclamatory rather
than expositional:

> O ignorant young creatures! How little do you know the effect of rack punch! What is the rack in the punch, at night, to the rack in the head of a morning?
>
> [THACKERAY, *Vanity Fair*, Ch. vi]

> Dead! Dead, your Majesty. Dead, my lords and gentlemen. Dead, Right Reverends and Wrong Reverends of every order. Dead, men and women, born with Heavenly compassion in your hearts. And dying around us every day.
>
> [DICKENS, *Bleak House*, Ch. xlvii]

> Poor Mr. Arabin – untaught, illiterate, boorish, ignorant man! That at forty years of age you should know so little of the workings of a woman's heart!
>
> [TROLLOPE, *Barchester Towers*, Ch. xxx

The above dissection has been achieved by concentrating on those novelists (and they include some of the greatest) who have kept the systems as separate stylistic strands in their novels. They move with deliberation and often with a noticeable change of prose from one system to the other. Not all novelists have accepted Fielding's simplicity and openness of texture. Sterne in this as in other ways runs counter to the eighteenth-century norm. In him the systems intertwine, even in a single sentence. Much of Jane Austen's originality lay in her multivalent use of prose. With her, dialogue could be implicit moralising; her characters are made self-revealing, without the overt intervention of the author – witness the opening chapter of *Sense and Sensibility*. Often what appears at first glance to be the uncomplicated sentence-structure of narrative contains commentary, buried in the syntax: the well-known narrative final sentence of Chapter 20 of *Mansfield Park* is also sharp commentary on the meanness of Mrs. Norris:

> The curtain over which she had presided with such talent and such success, went off with her to her cottage, where she happened to be particularly in need of green baize.

Jane Austen offers no comment here in her own persona. The condemnation of Mrs. Norris is done by the author's manipulation of the syntax – the contrived but apparently innocent placing of the final clause, the choice of 'the curtain' and not 'Mrs. Norris' as the grammatical subject, and the use of the verb 'went' in the main clause – the curtain simply 'went' with her to her cottage, as if (ironically) *it* and not Mrs. Norris had made the decision.

Though it was to be many years before their lead was followed, it was Sterne and Jane Austen who were the main initiators in what has become the most important modern development of prose in fiction. Writings as diverse as *The Ambassadors* (1903), *Ulysses* (1922), *The Doll's House* (1923), and *The Catcher in the Rye* (1951) represent a new attitude and a new use of prose which is extremely common in the present-day novel. The voice of the author, in his own persona as narrator, commentator and the rest, has finally disappeared. The author contrives to sink himself entirely in the character he presents. Everything is seen through his eyes – and presented in his speech. James, who formulated this new insistence on a 'point of view' inside the novel, would have recoiled at some of the consequences which have ensued e.g. the presentation of the narrative through childish syntax or illiterate speech-forms. But its success is demonstrable.

The shift to an internal point of view has had a further consequence, which has been exploited with equal success. Sterne's replacement of the syntax of speech with a verbal transcription of the movement of thought has opened the way to what has become the fifth prose 'system' in the novel, the interior monologue. This presentation of inner thought through a 'stream of consciousness' has been tackled in various ways, each of them an attempt at setting down the non-syntactic 'language' of free association. A series of linked images expressed as a pattern of noun phrases (Dos Passos); a long sequence of short speech-based sentences and exclamatory phrases running into each other without punctuation (the final section of *Ulysses*); a discursive 'sentence' made up of a series of loosely linked clauses designed to echo the ebb and flow of reminiscence (William Faulkner); these have all proved to be effective.

It is likely that the writers of the 1920's thought of themselves as creating a new form of the novel; in a novel like *To the Lighthouse* (1927) the four earlier prose systems are entirely supplanted by a series of interior monologues. But readers have come speedily to accept what was only a few years ago a difficult innovation; and the interior monologue, with its range of non-syntactic devices, is now no more than a fifth prose system open to any novelist – and, indeed, to most readers. No more convincing demonstration could be found of the expansion of the reading public discussed in the previous chapter. Sterne's innovations appealed in his own day and for many subsequent years to a small minority of readers. Today the writer of widely popular fiction has all five prose systems at his command and even the detective novelist can move from speech-based narrative to the disrupted syntax of the interior monologue, in the firm expectation that the most casual reader will accept.

Discussion Section

1. 'Words like 'sad', 'silly', 'shrewd', 'domination', 'gentle', 'smoke', 'wit', 'sentence', all in good present-day usage with precise and specific meanings, have carried very different meanings in past centuries.' (Chap. 1, p. 6.)

   (a) What meanings have these words carried in the past?
   (b) Do these earlier meanings have any influence on the usage of the words today?

2. Read Chapter 2 and Appendix A. With the aid of an etymological dictionary, identify the native words [i.e. those derived from Old English] and the words borrowed from other languages in the Milton passage on page 107.
   What is the percentage of foreign words in the passage:

   (a) on a vocabulary basis (counting each word only once, irrespective of the number of times it occurs)?
   (b) on an occurrence basis (counting every word every time it occurs)?

   What deductions can you make from your results? Choose a passage of comparable length from a newspaper, and repeat both calculations.
   What is the significance of any differences you discover?

3. Using the symbols described on page 21, mark the stresses and 'boundary-markers' in the following passage from T. L. Peacock:

   THE REV. DR. FOLLIOTT. Sir, Diderot is not a man after my heart. Keep to the Greeks, if you please; albeit this Sleeping Venus is not an antique.
   MR. CROTCHET. Well, sir, the Greeks: why do we call the Elgin marbles inestimable? Simply because they are true to nature. And why are they so superior in that point to all modern works, with all our greater knowledge of anatomy? Why, sir, because the Greeks, having no cant, had better opportunity of studying models?
   THE REV. DR. FOLLIOTT. Sir, I deny our greater knowledge of anatomy.

4. The following passage is from Chaucer's *Parson's Tale*. The spelling has

been slightly modernised. How far does the structure of Chaucer's sentences in this passage correspond to that of Modern English? In what ways does it differ?

> Now cometh idle words, that is withouten profit of him that speketh tho [those] words, and eke of him that herkeneth tho words. Or else idle words been tho that been needless, or withouten entente of natural profit. And al be it that idle words been sometime venial sin, yet should men douten [doubt] them, for we should give rekenynge of them before God.

5. The following two passages were written towards the end of the fifteenth century. Account for the differences in vocabulary and sentence-structure.

(a) Behind this gate is there another spire of stone more noble than that other, graven with diverse sculptures. Among all, there is wrought the mortal war and battle that was against the Bactians whom this king's sons had under their dominion that did this deed at his commandment against this people with four hundred thousand men afoot and twenty thousand spearmen, so that the field was divided in four parts when he took his journey forward. [mod. sp.]

(b) So at the laste they wente into the shippe all three, and founde hit rychely behanged with cloth of sylke. So by that tyme hit was durke nyght, there suddeynly was aboute them an hondred torchis sette uppon all the shyppe-bordis, and hit gaff grete lyght. And there-withall there come twelve fayre damesels and salued kynge Arthure on hir kneis, and called hym be his name and seyde he was ryght wellcom, and suche chere as they had he sholde have of the beste. Than the kynge thanked hem fayre. Therewythall they ledde the kynge and his felawys into a fayre chambir, and there was a clothe leyde richely beseyne of all that longed to a table, and there were they served of all wynes and metys that they coude thynke of. But of that the kynge had grete mervayle, for he never fared bettir in his lyff as for one souper.

6. The following two passages are from books which were published in 1594. Account for the differences in vocabulary and sentence-structure. Do they have any features in common?

(a) Now if nature should intermit her course, and leave altogether though it were but for a while the observation of her own laws; if those principal and mother elements of the world, whereof all things in this lower world are made, should lose the qualities which now they have; if the frame of that heavenly arch erected over our heads should loosen and dissolve itself; if celestial spheres should forget their wonted motions, and by irregular volubility turn themselves any way as it might happen; if the prince of the lights of heaven, which now as a giant doth run his unwearied course, should as it were through a languishing faintness begin to stand and to rest himself; if the moon should wander from her beaten way, the times and seasons of the year blend themselves by disordered and confused mixture, the winds breathe out their last gasp, the clouds yield no rain, the earth be defeated of heavenly influence, the fruits of the earth pine away as children at the withered breasts of their mother no longer able to yield them relief: what would become of man himself, whom these things now do all serve? See we not plainly that obedience of creatures unto the law of nature is the stay of the whole world?

(b) There was a Lord in the campe, let him be a Lord of misrule if you will, for he kept a plaine alehouse without welt or gard of anie iuybush, and sold syder and cheese by pint and by pound to all that came (at the verie name of sider I can but sigh, there is so much of it in renish wine now a daies.) Well, *Tendit ad sydera virtus*, thers great vertue belongs (I can tel you) to a cup of sider, and very good men haue sold it, and at sea it is *Aqua coelestis*, but thats neither here nor there, if it had no other patrone but this peere of quart pottes to authorize it, it were sufficient. This great Lord, this worthie Lord, this noble Lord, thought no scorne (Lord haue mercie vpon us) to haue his great veluet breeches larded with the droppinges of this daintie liquor, & yet he was an old seruitor, a cauelier of an ancient house, as might appeare by the armes of his ancestors drawen verie amiably in chalke on the inside of his tent dore.

7. Using the Authorised Version, compare Genesis 27 (verses 1-17) and Jeremiah 9 (verses 1-11). Account for differences in linguistic features (e.g. vocabulary, latinisms, rhetorical figures, imagery). What elements have they in common?

8. Analyse the sentence-structure of the passage (which was published in 1641) printed on page 107.
    In what ways does this differ from the sentence-structure of the following passage (which was published in 1605)?

But the greatest error of all the rest is the mistaking or misplacing of the last or farthest end of knowledge: for men have entered into a desire of learning and knowledge, sometimes upon a natural curiosity and inquisitive appetite; sometimes to entertain their minds with variety and delight; sometimes for ornament and reputation; and sometimes to enable them to victory of wit and contradiction; and most times for lucre and profession; and seldom sincerely to give a true account of their gift of reason, to the benefit and use of men: as if there were sought in knowledge a couch whereupon to rest a searching and restless spirit; or a tarrasse, for a wandering and variable mind to walk up and down with a fair prospect; or a tower of state, for a proud mind to raise itself upon; or a fort or commanding ground, for strife and contention; or a shop, for profit or sale; and not a rich storehouse, for the glory of the Creator and the relief of man's estate.

Why should the earlier passage appear to be closer to modern prose?

9. Compare the passage from Donne on page 118 with the following passage on a similar theme by Jeremy Taylor (published shortly after the Donne passage):

It is a thing that everyone suffers, even persons of the lowest resolution, of the meanest virtue, of no breeding, of no discourse. Take away but the pomps of death, the disguises and solemn bugbears, the tinsel, and the actings by candle-light, and proper and fantastic ceremonies, the minstrels and the noise-makers, the women and the weepers, the swoonings and the shriekings, the nurses and the physicians, the dark room and the ministers, the kindred and the watchers; and then to die is easy, ready, and quitted from its troublesome circumstances. It is the same harmless thing, that a poor shepherd suffered yesterday, or a maid-servant to-day; and at the same time in which you die, in that very night a thousand creatures die with you, some wise men, and many fools; and the wisdom of the first will not quit him, and the folly of the latter does not make him unable to die.

What differences and similarities are there in sentence-structure, imagery, and rhetorical figures?

What evidence can you find in one passage or the other to suggest that it is a transcript of spoken prose?

10. The following passage is from Addison's first *Spectator* (1711):

I have passed my latter Years in this City, where I am frequently seen in most publick Places, tho' there are not above half a dozen of my select Friends that know me, of whom my next Paper shall give a more particular Account. There is no place of general Resort, wherein I do not often make my appearance; sometimes I am seen thrusting my Head into a Round of Politicians at *Will's*, and listning with great Attention to the Narratives that are made in those little Circular Audiences. Sometimes I smoak a Pipe at *Child's*; and whilst I seem attentive to nothing but the *Post-Man*, over-hear the Conversation of every Table in the Room. I appear on *Sunday* nights at St. *James's* Coffee-House, and sometimes join the little Committee of Politicks in the Inner Room, as one who comes there to hear and improve. My Face is likewise very well known at the *Grecian*, the *Cocoa-Tree*, and in the Theatres both of *Drury-Lane* and the *Hay-Market*. I have been taken for a Merchant upon the *Exchange* for above these ten Years, and sometimes pass for a *Jew* in the Assembly of Stock-Jobbers at *Jonathan's*. In short, where-ever I see a Cluster of People I always mix with them, though I never open my Lips but in my own Club.

To what extent do you think the above passage renders 'real speech'? Where in this passage does Addison use phrases or structures unlikely to be heard in conversation?

11. Select a page from a prose play written between 1660 and the end of the eighteenth century (e.g. Congreve, Goldsmith, Sheridan). Select a page that is predominantly dialogue from a novel by an eighteenth century novelist (e.g. Fielding, Smollett, Fanny Burney). What differences do you observe between conversation written to be read and conversation written to be actually spoken?

12. The following three extracts are all by Dr. Johnson: (a) is from a private letter to Mrs. Thrale, (b) is from the Preface to his Dictionary, (c) is from his conversation as recorded by Boswell. What similarities and differences do they exhibit?

(a) Dear Madam

Such tattle as filled your last sweet Letter prevents one great inconvenience of absence, that of returning home a stranger and an enquirer. The variations of life consist of little things. Important innovations are soon heard, and easily understood. Men that meet to talk of Physicks or Metaphysicks, or law or history may be immediately acquainted. We look at each other in silence only for want of petty talk upon slight occurrences. Continue therefore to write all that You would say.

(b) When I first collected these authorities, I was desirous that every quotation should be useful to some other end than the illustration of a word; I therefore extracted from philosophers principles of science; from historians remarkable facts; from chymists complete processes; from divines striking exhortations; and from poets beautiful descriptions. Such is design, while it is yet at a distance from execution. When the time called upon me to range this accumulation of elegance and wisdom into an alphabetical series, I soon discovered that the bulk of my volumes would fright away the student, and was forced to depart from my scheme of including all that was pleasing or useful in *English* literature, and reduce my transcripts very often to clusters of words, in which scarcely any meaning is retained; thus to the weariness of copying, I was condemned to add the vexation of expunging. Some passages I have yet spared, which may relieve the labour of verbal searches, and intersperse with verdure and flowers the dusty desarts of barren philology.

(c) Talking of the effects of drinking, he said, 'Drinking may be practised with great prudence; a man who exposes himself when he is intoxicated, has not the art of getting drunk; a sober man who happens occasionally to get drunk, readily enough goes into a new company, which a man who has been drinking should never do. Such a man will undertake any thing; he is without skill in inebriation. I used to slink home when I had drunk too much.'

13. The following two extracts were written by scientists, (a) in the nineteenth century, (b) in the twentieth. In what ways do they differ from scientific prose written in the late seventeenth century (e.g. the passage from Boyle on page 128)?

(a) Again, think of the microscopic fungus – a mere infinitesimal ovoid particle, which finds space and duration enough to multiply in countless millions in the body of a living fly; and then of the wealth of foliage, the luxuriance of flower and fruit, which lies between this bald sketch of a plant and the giant pine of California, towering to the dimensions of a cathedral spire, or the Indian fig, which covers acres with its profound shadow, and endures while nations and empires come and go around its vast circumference. Or, turning to the other half of the world of life, picture to yourselves the great Finner whale, hugest of beasts that live, or have lived, disporting his eighty or ninety feet of bone, muscle, and blubber, with easy roll, among waves in which the stoutest ship that ever left dockyard would founder hopelessly; and contrast him with the invisible animalcules – mere gelatinous specks, multitudes of which could, in fact, dance upon the point of a needle with the same ease as the angels of the Schoolmen could, in imagination. With these images before your minds, you may well ask, what community of form, or structure, is there between the animalcule and the whale; or between the fungus and the fig-tree? And, *a fortiori*, between all four?

(b) The causes which lead to the disintegration of the atom are at present a matter of conjecture. It is not yet possible to decide with certainty whether the disintegration is due to an external cause, or is an inherent property of the atom itself. It is conceivable, for example, that some unknown external force may supply the necessary disturbance to cause disintegration. In such a case, the external force supplies the place of a detonator to precipitate the atomic explosion. The energy liberated by the explosion, however, is derived mainly from the atom itself and not from the detonator. The law of transformation of radioactive matter does not throw any light on the question, for such a law is to be expected on either hypothesis.

What features of romantic prose are contained in extract (a)? Why are they there?

Examine recent examples of prose written by scientists, and analyse their prose in terms of the three 'styles' discussed at the end of Chapter 13. What is the value to a scientific writer of romantic prose?

14. What features of mid-nineteenth-century romantic prose are contained in the following passages? How effective are they?

(a) She gave him her hand, her little fair hand: there was only her marriage ring on it. The quarrel was all over. The year of grief and estrangement was passed. They never had been separated. His mistress had never been out of his mind all that time. No, not once, No, not in the prison; nor in the camp; nor on shore before the enemy; nor at sea under the stars of solemn midnight, nor as he watched the glorious rising of the dawn: not even at the table, where he sat carousing with friends, or at the theatre yonder, where he tried to fancy that other eyes were brighter than hers. Brighter eyes there might be, and faces more beautiful, but none so dear – no voice so sweet as that of his beloved mistress, who had been sister, mother, goddess to him during his youth – goddess now no more, for he knew of her weaknesses; and by thought, by suffering, and that experience it brings, was older now than she; but more fondly cherished as woman perhaps than ever she had been adored as divinity. What is it? Where lies it? the secret which makes one little hand the dearest of all? Whoever can unriddle that mystery? Here she was, her son by his side, his dear boy. Here she was, weeping and happy. (1852)

(b) There is an advertisement in the papers announcing a building project at Wimbledon and Westhill. The houses are to occupy a portion of Wimbledon Park; and boards are put among the trees by the roadside, boasting of the 'fine frontage'. Well may they boast of it, especially at this season of the year. It is a golden undulation; a foreground, and from some points of view, a middle distance, fit to make the richest painter despair; a veritable Field of Cloth of Gold. Morning (Aurora, the golden goddess), when the dawn is of a fineness to match, must look beauty for beauty on it. Sunset is divine. The gold goes stretching away in the distance towards the dark trees, like the rich evening of a poetic life. (1851)

(c) I cannot but notice, in speaking to gentlemen who sit on either side of this House, or in speaking to anyone I meet between this House and any of those localities we frequent when this House is up – I cannot, I say, but notice that an uneasy feeling exists as to the news that may arrive by the very next mail from the East. I do not suppose that your troops are to be beaten in actual conflict with the foe, or that they will be driven into the sea; but I am certain that many homes in England in which there now exists a fond hope that the distant one may return – many such homes will be rendered desolate when the next mail shall arrive. The angel of death has been abroad throughout the land; you may almost hear the beating of his wings. There is no one, as when the first-born were slain of old, to sprinkle with blood the lintel and the two sideposts of our doors, that he may spare and pass on: he takes his victims from the castle of the noble, the mansion of the wealthy, and the cottage of the poor and lowly, and it is on behalf of all these classes that I make this solemn appeal. (1855)

15. Partly owing to copyright problems, and partly owing to the space needed for long extracts, no passages from novels are included. The following topics are suggested for discussion, which should relate to *specific* texts, not to general memories of works read.

(a) How far has the 'extended speech-range' (see Chapter 16, page 162) contributed to the success of American and English novels published since 1940?

(b) 'Where the narrator is a persona other than the author, the general solution until quite recently has been to retain the author's voice.' (Chapter 16, page 163)

Examine the effect in a recent novel where the 'voice' of the narrator is not that of the author.

(c) How far is the use of romantic prose for 'background and scenery' (Chapter 16, page 164) still a feature of contemporary fiction?

(d) 'Today the writer of widely popular fiction has all five prose systems at his command.' (Chapter 16, page 167)

Which of the five 'systems' appear to be the most prominent (and the most effective) in recent fiction?

16. Other topics for discussion:

'[Romantic prose] continues with unabated vigour an extra-literary life in the special world of advertising.' Check the validity of this assertion by collecting and studying the syntactic, metaphoric, and other devices used in newspaper and magazine advertising.

Collect some hundreds of newspaper headlines. From these deduce the syntax of the newspaper headline. In what ways does this differ from the syntax of ordinary narrative prose?

What differences, if any, can you discover between the prose of the daily newspaper, and the prose of the weeklies?

With the use of a tape-recorder, transcribe 300 words of 'ordinary' unscripted conversation. Try to transcribe all pauses, 'ums' and 'ers', as well as actual words. Do not 'edit' it in any way. How far does what you have transcribed correspond to the 'movement of conversation' as recorded in a novel? What are the differences?

Further Reading

This section is designed for the non-specialist reader. A full bibliography of critical and analytical writings on English prose would demand a book in itself.

The basic reading, at all times, should be the actual texts of authors. There is much valuable material in the standard literary histories and in the critical introductions to the major editions of prose authors. The advanced student of literature and of language (though less so of linguistics) will require at all points to consult the Cambridge Bibliography of English Literature and follow the leads given there and in the specialist studies it enumerates.

In addition to works already cited in the notes, the following list (highly selective and mainly on the formative years of the modern period) can be recommended.

H. S. BENNETT, 'Science and Information in English Writings of the Fifteenth Century', *Mod. Lang. Review* 39, 1944.

H. S. BENNETT, 'Fifteenth Century Secular Prose', *Rev. Eng. Studies*, 21, 1945.

H. S. BENNETT, *English Books and Readers 1475–1557*, Cambridge, 1952.

JOAN BENNETT, 'An Aspect of the Evolution of Seventeenth Century Prose', *RES*, 17, 1941.

H. CRAIK (ed.) *English Prose*, 5 vols., London, 1893.

W. C. CRANE, *Wit and Rhetoric in the Renaissance*, New York, 1937.

M. W. CROLL, 'The Cadence of English Oratorical Prose', *Studies in Philology*, xvi, 1919.

M. W. CROLL, ' "Attic Prose" in the Seventeenth Century', *Studies in Philology*, xviii, 1921.

M. W. CROLL, 'The Baroque Style in Prose', *Studies in English Philology*, ed. K. Malone and M. B. Ruud, Minneapolis, 1929.

B. DOBRÉE, *Modern Prose Style*, Oxford, 1964 (2nd. ed.)

R. F. JONES, 'The Attack on Pulpit Eloquence in the Restoration', *Journal of English and Germanic Philology*, 30, 1931.

R. F. JONES (and others), *The Seventeenth Century, Studies in the History of English Thought*, Stanford, 1951.

R. F. JONES, *The Triumph of the English Language*, Stanford, 1953.

H. MACDONALD, 'Another Aspect of Seventeenth Century Prose', *RES*, 30, 1941.

H. READ, *English Prose Style*, London, 1942.

A. C. SOUTHERN, *Elizabethan Recusant Prose*, London, 1950.

B. M. H. STRANG, *Modern English Structure*, London, 1962.

J. R. SUTHERLAND, 'Some Aspects of Eighteenth Century Prose', *Essays on the Eighteenth Century*, Presented to David Nichol Smith, Oxford, 1945.

J. R. SUTHERLAND, *On English Prose*, Toronto, 1957.

E. J. SWEETING, *Early Tudor Criticism*, Oxford, 1940.

H. B. WHITEHALL, *Structural Essentials of English*, New York, 1956.

G. WILLIAMSON, 'Senecan Style in the Seventeenth Century', *Philological Quarterly*, 15, 1936.

G. WILLIAMSON, *The Senecan Amble*, London, 1951.

F. P. WILSON, *Seventeenth Century Prose*, Cambridge, 1960.

W. K. WIMSATT, *The Prose Style of Samuel Johnson*, New Haven, 1941.

S. K. WORKMAN, *Fifteenth Century Translation as an Influence on English Prose*, Princeton, 1940.

Index

The index lists, under authors' names and (for mediaeval and some other works) titles, only those references where there is some commentary or discussion in the text.